AF483682

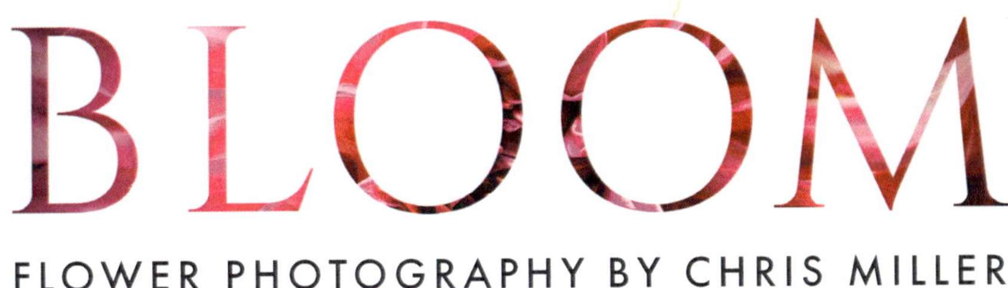

FLOWER PHOTOGRAPHY BY CHRIS MILLER

*For my Dad, who worked
tirelessly to put food — and
flowers — on the table.*

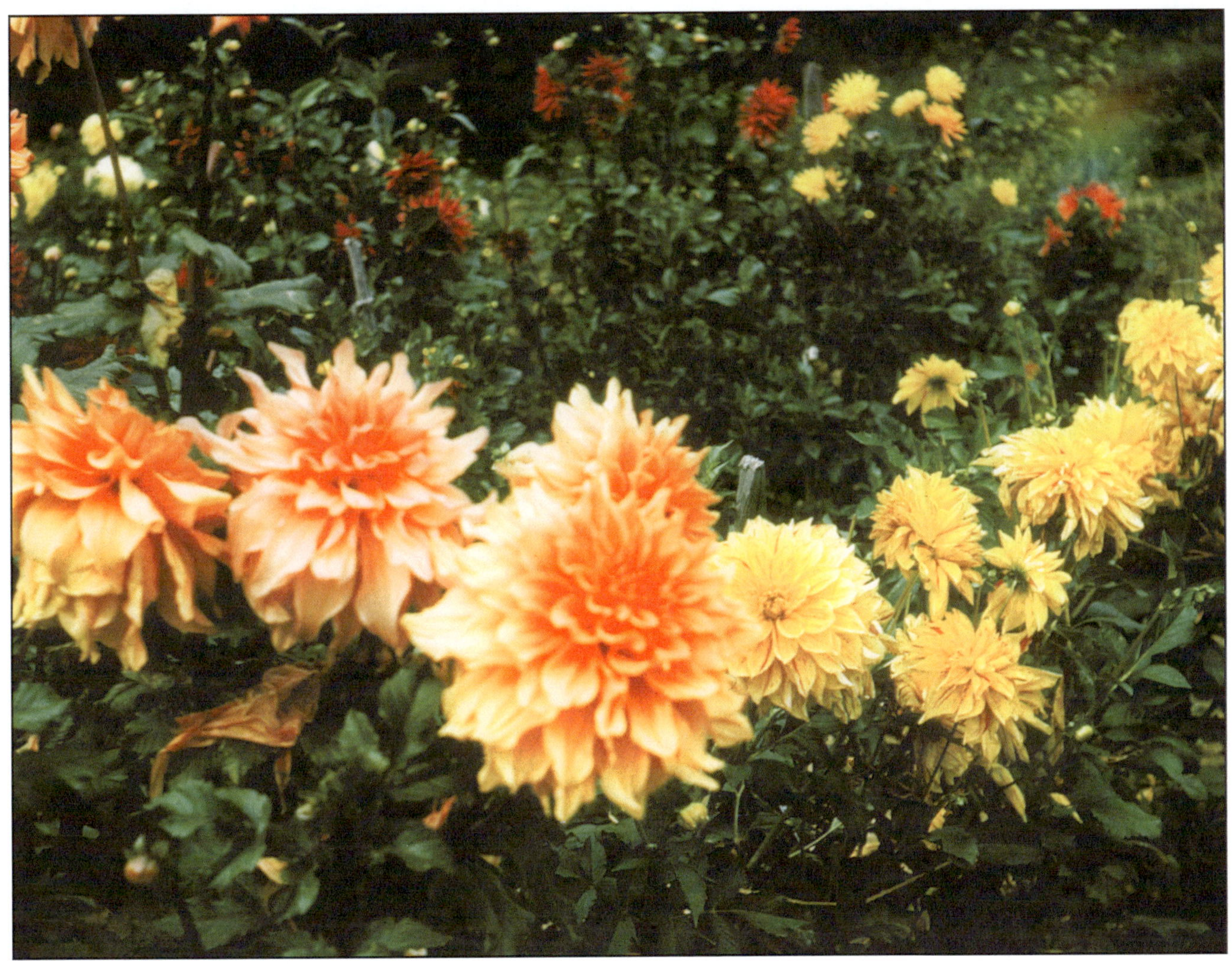

Family dahlia garden, sometime in the 1960s.

I was the youngest of my family. Dahlias, among a few
other things, preceded me. My earliest memories involve
dahlias towering tall over my head. Growing them is a
family tradition that lives on. In my garden, my sister's
garden, and in my sister-in-law's garden. They serve as
living memories of my dad, my mom, and my brother.

I've grown them my entire adult life whenever possible.
I became fascinated with capturing their symmetry and
beauty to enjoy after their three-month season.

Of course those qualities are not afforded to dahlias alone,
so it's natural that my project moved on to other flowers.

Family memories aside, there is a life lesson in putting
a dessicated little turd in the ground and waiting.
For copious amounts of rain in the Pacific Northwest.
For long-awaited sun. And after a while, from that little
tuber comes a few tiny leaves that turn into significant
stalks, and eventually the plant explodes in color.

All in good time. Much like with humans. We all need the
right conditions — and time — to bloom.

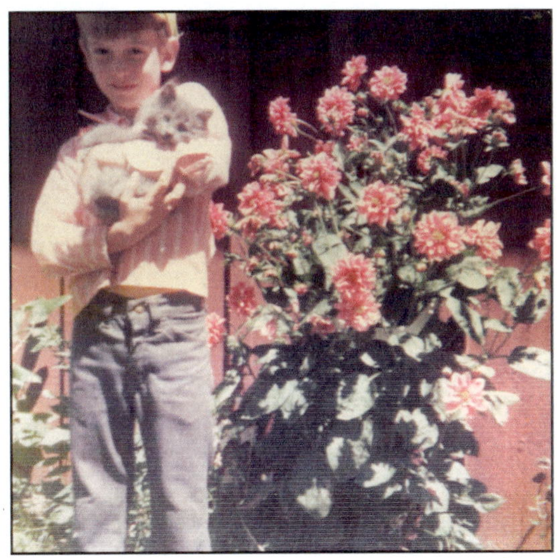

Me with feline friend and dahlias, mid-70's.

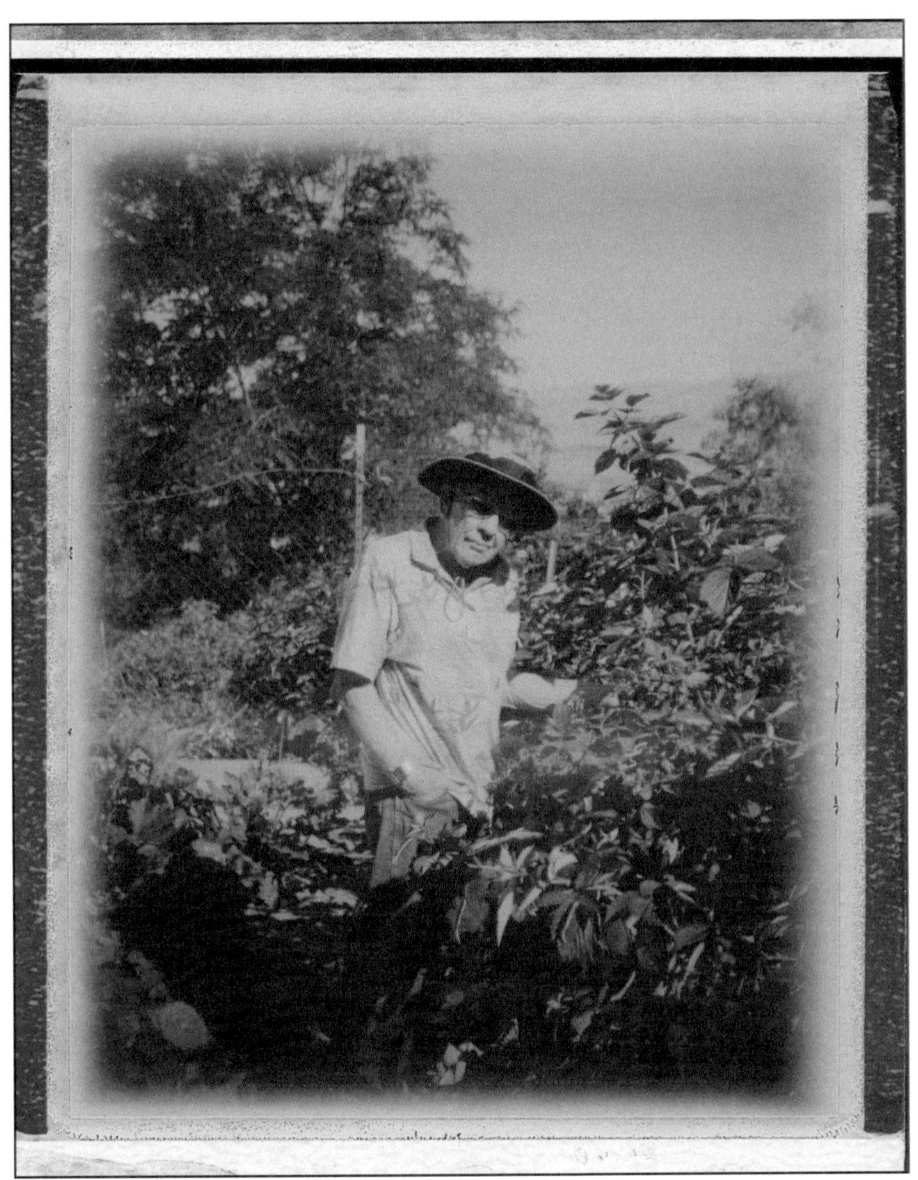

My Dad in his garden, 2018. He passed in 2019.

PLATES

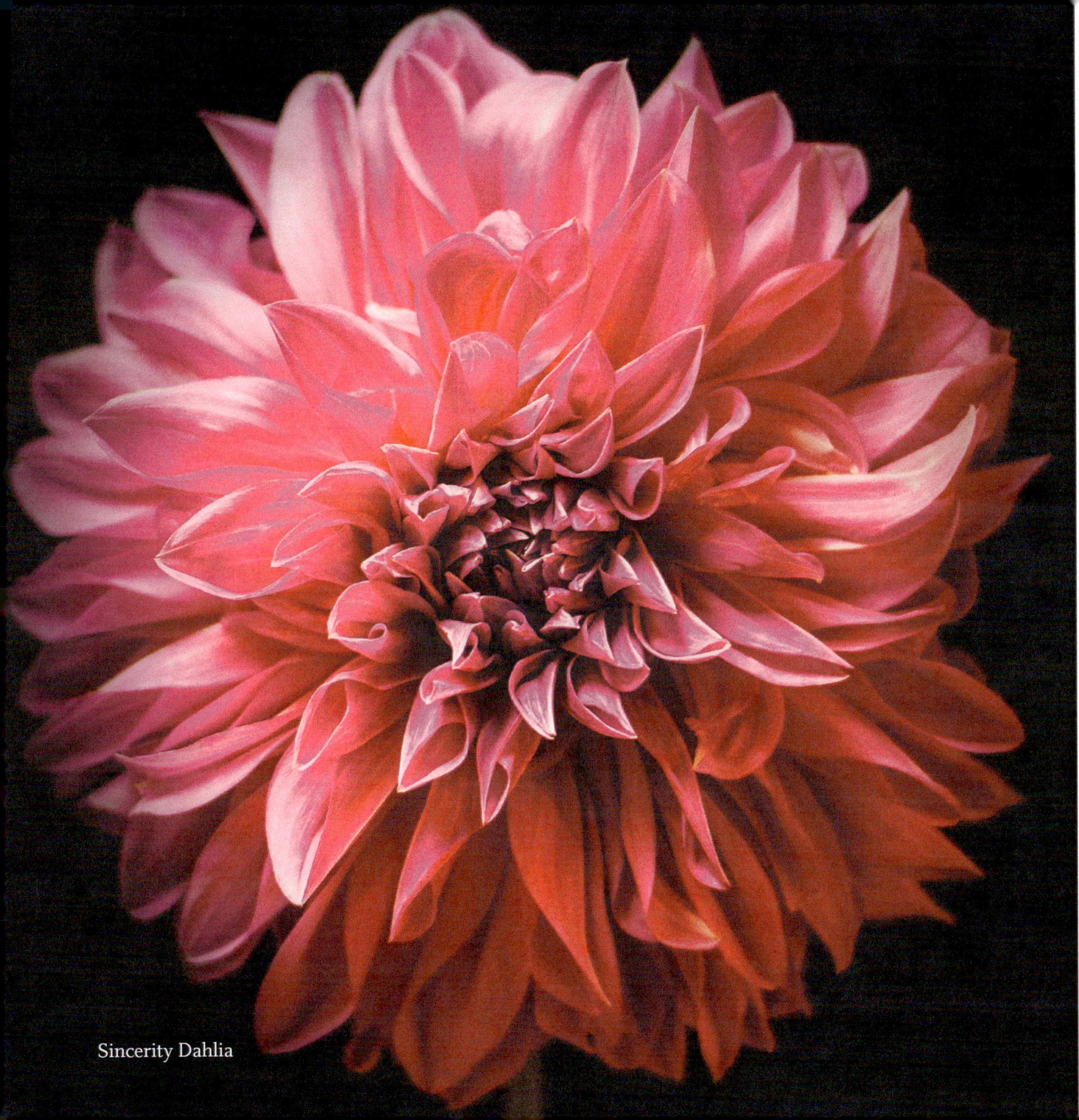

Sincerity Dahlia

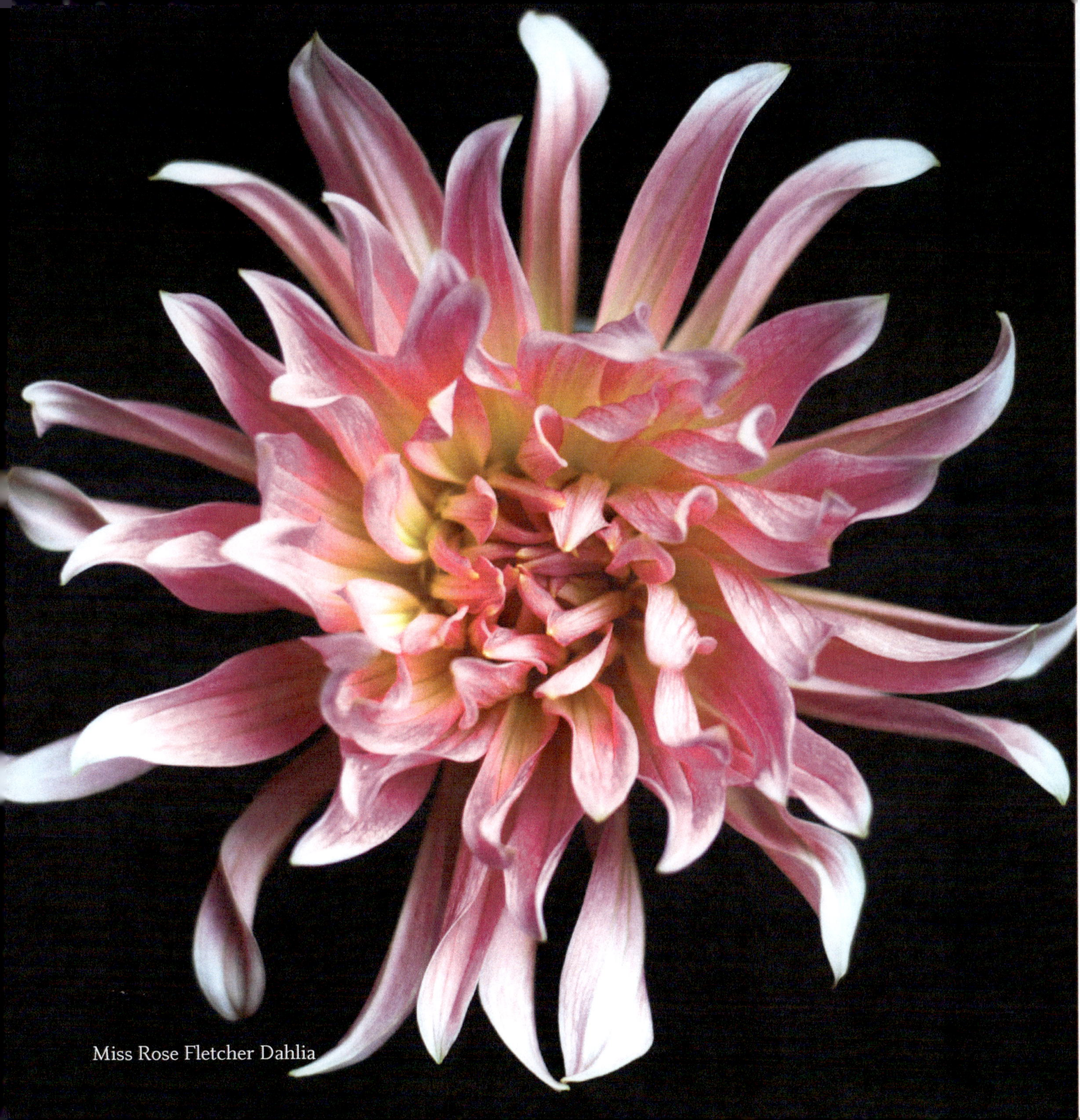

Miss Rose Fletcher Dahlia

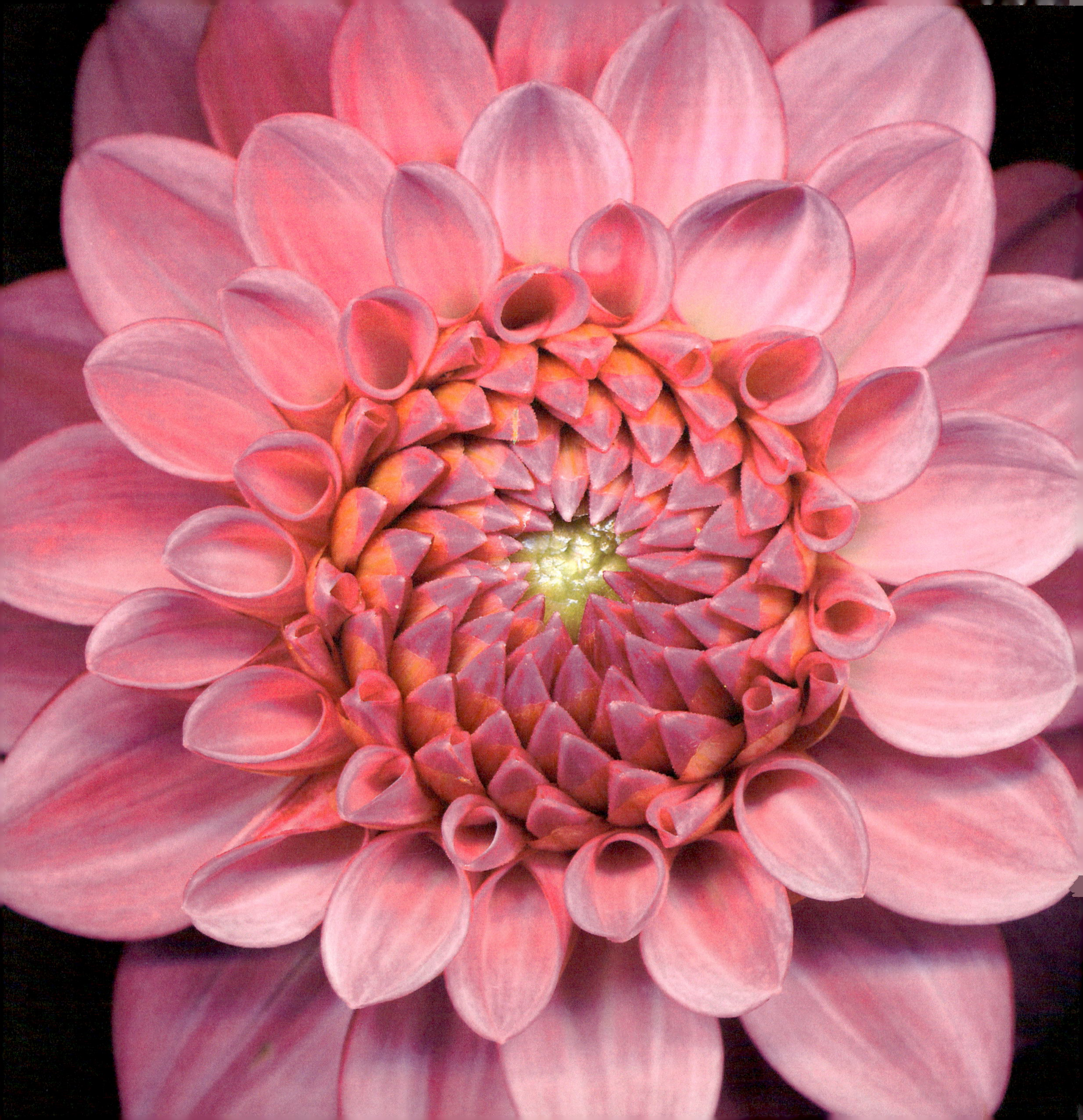

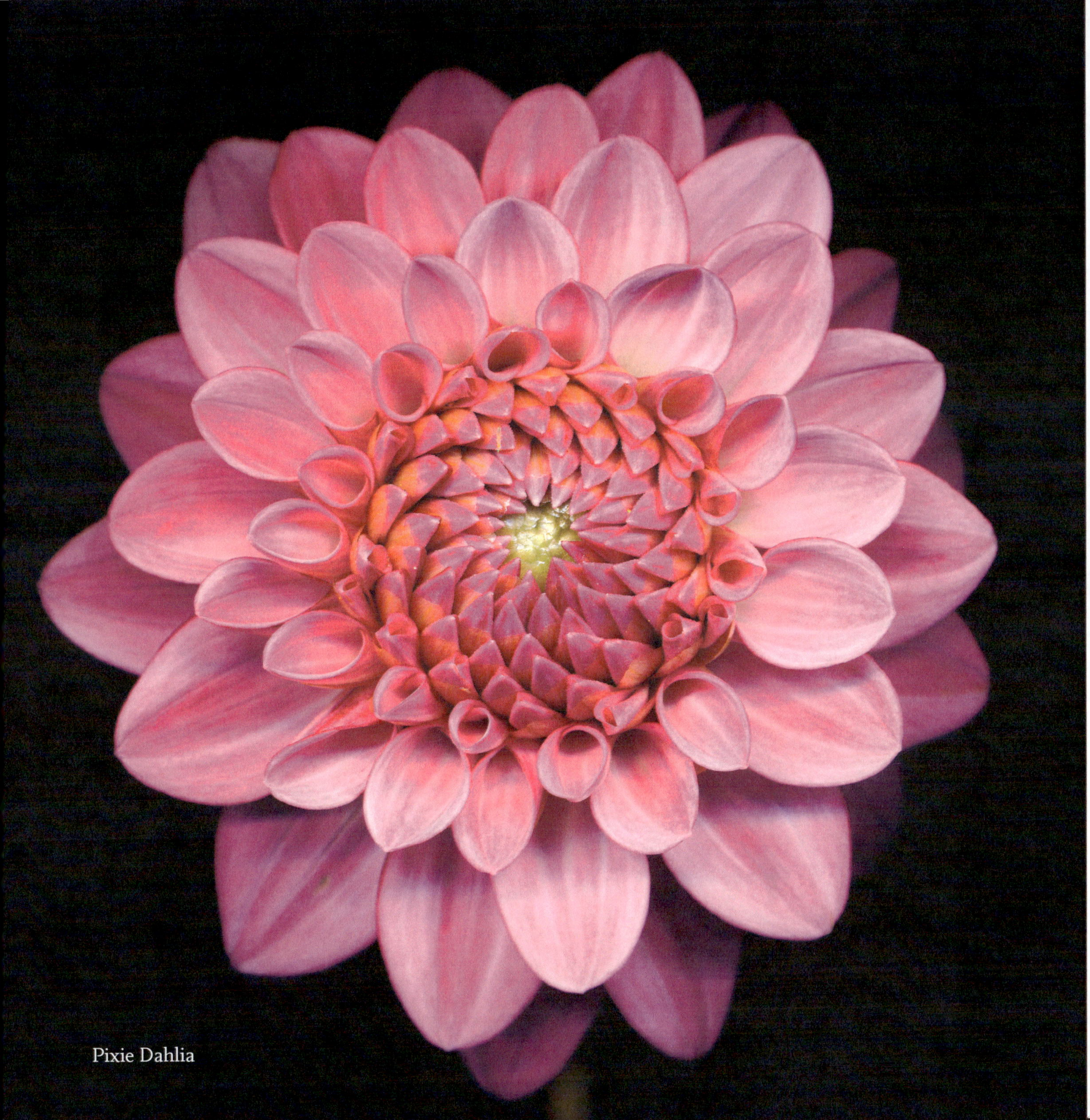
Pixie Dahlia

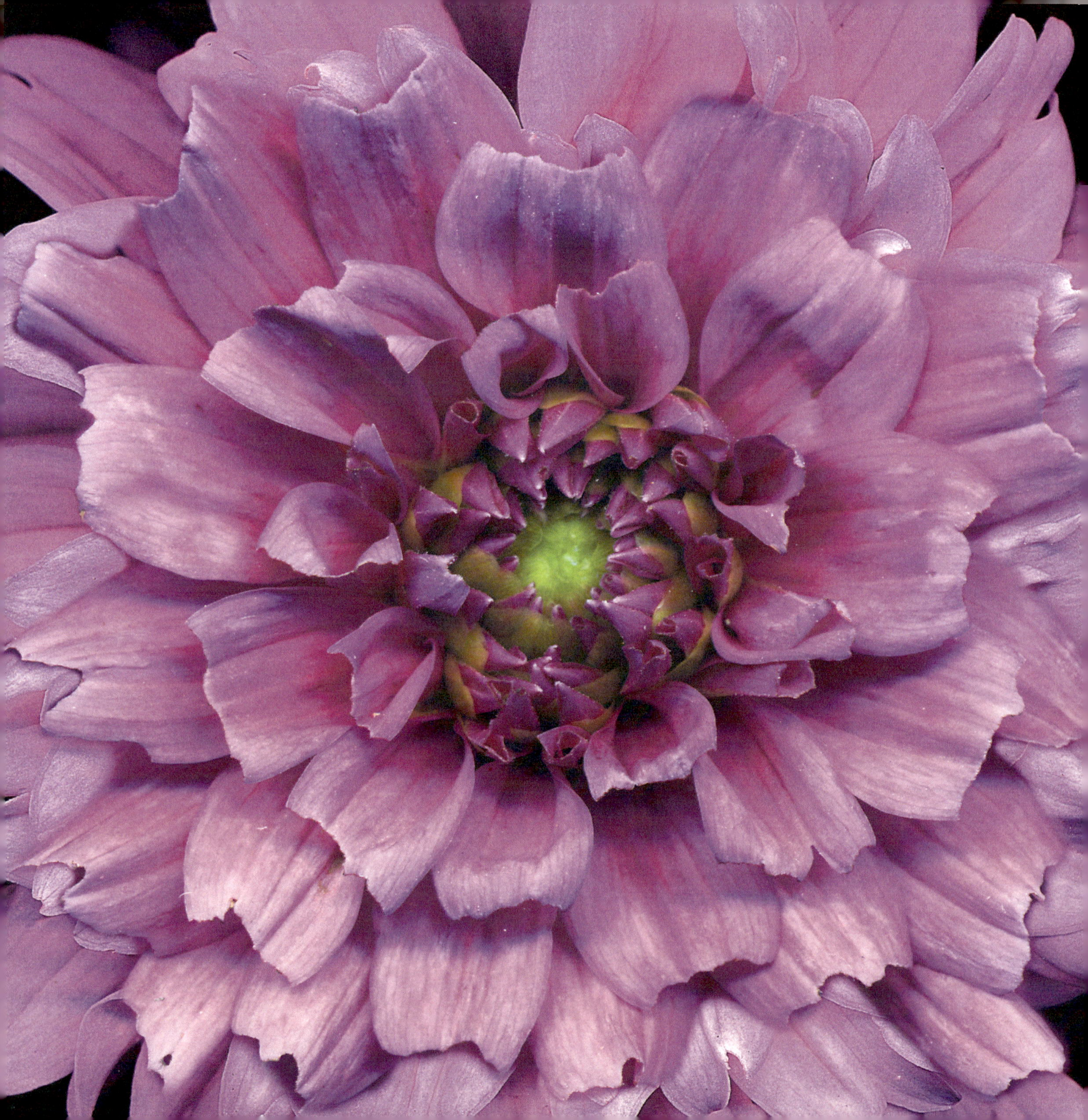

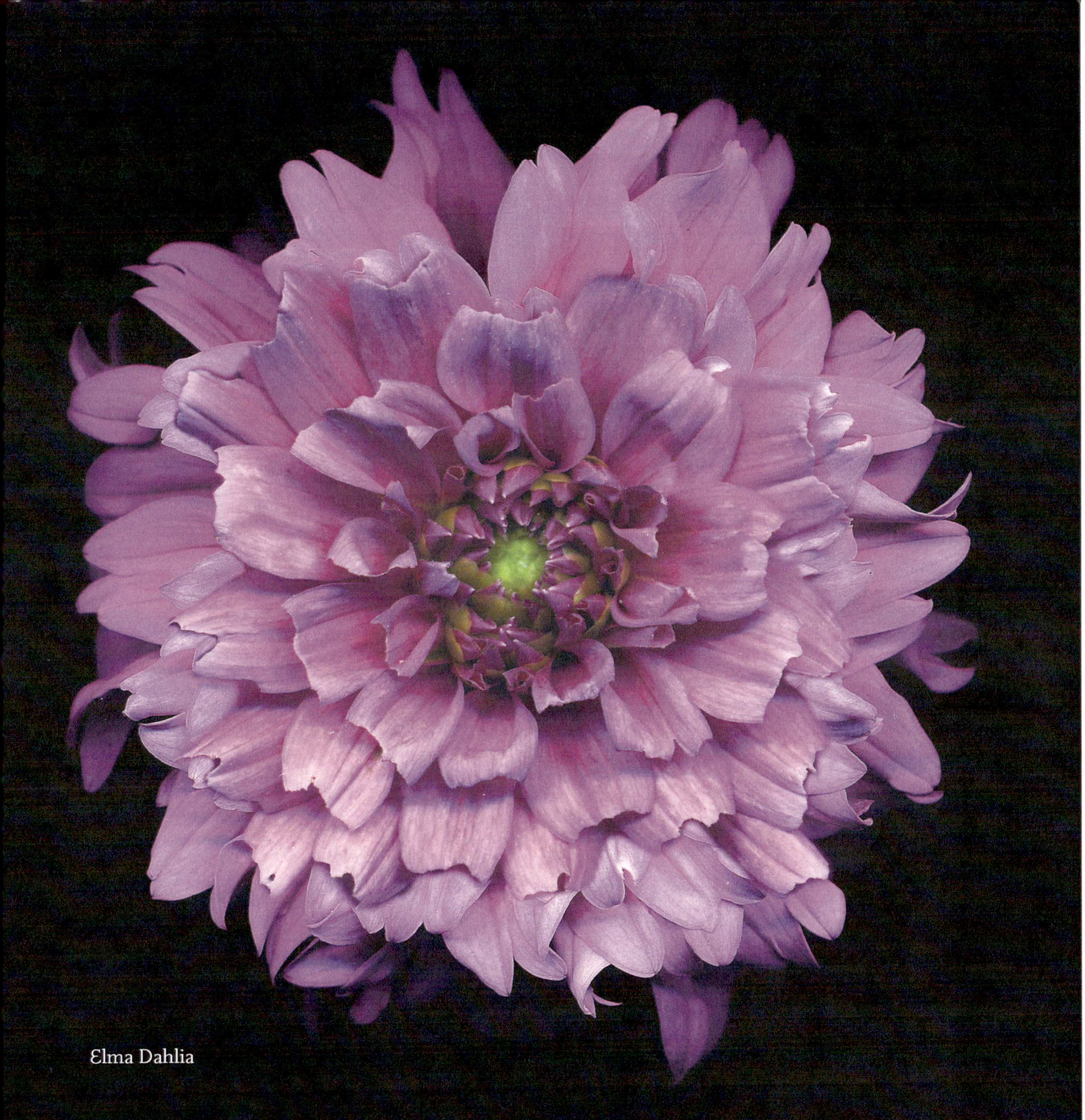
Elma Dahlia

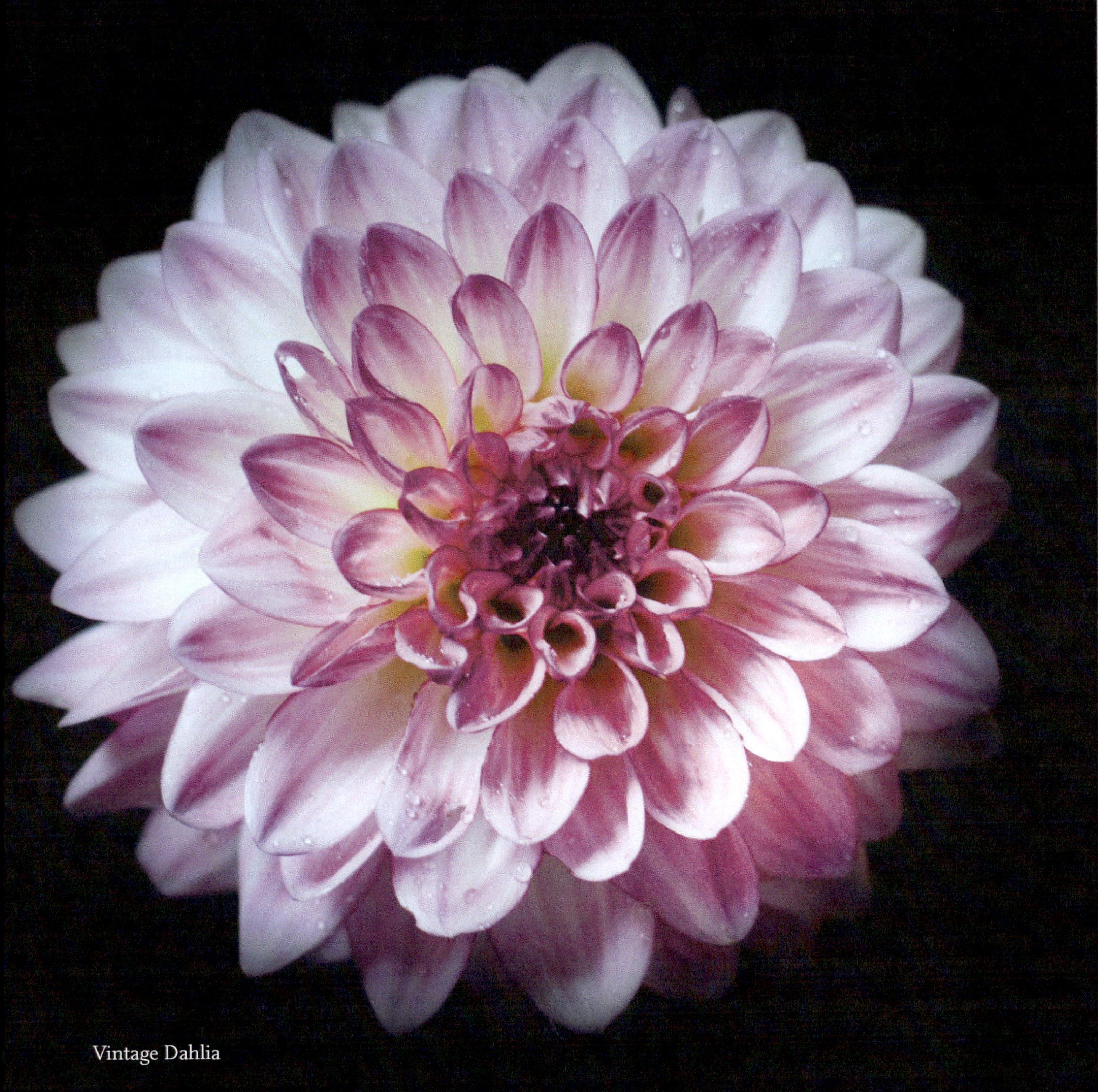
Vintage Dahlia

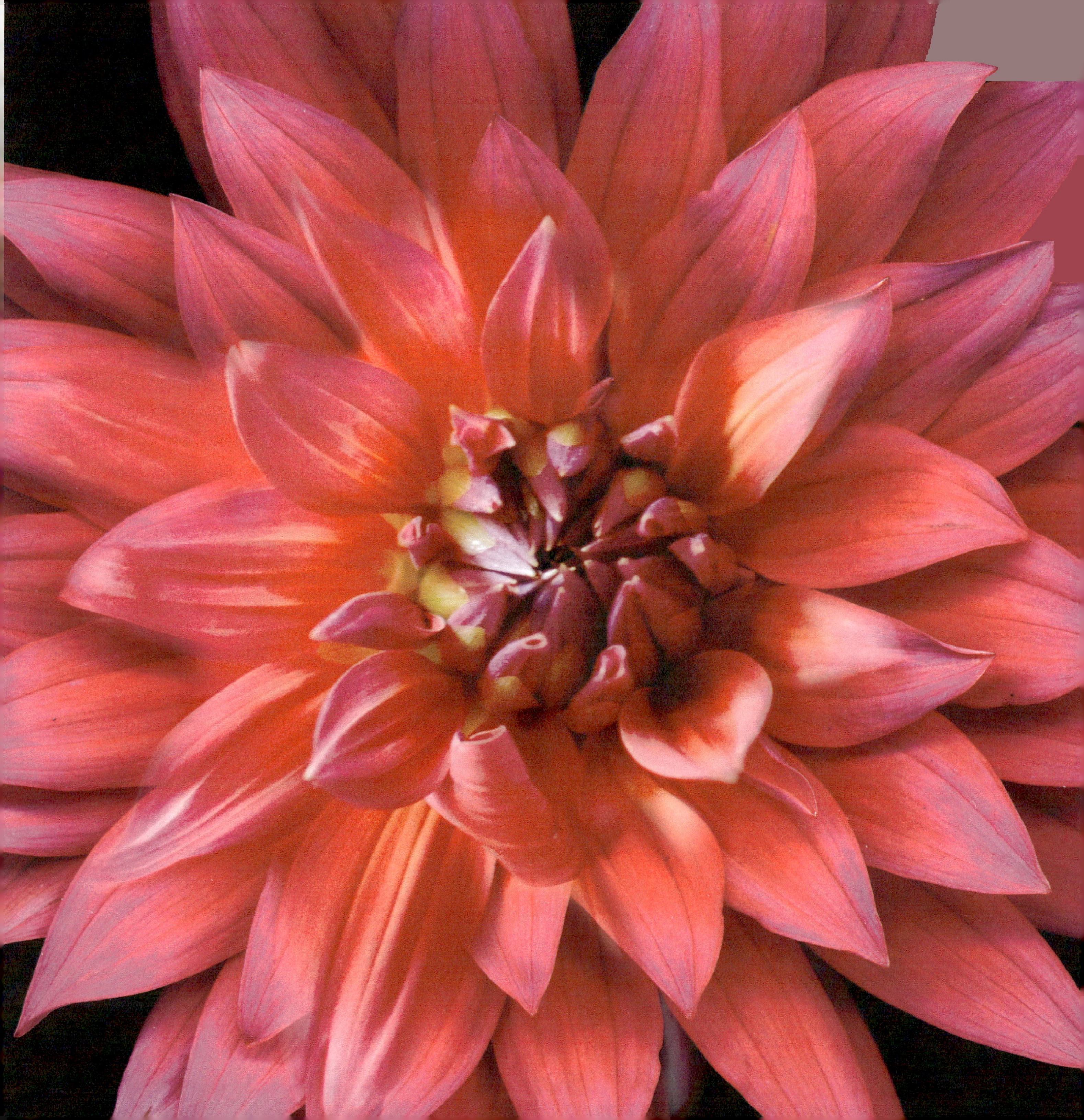

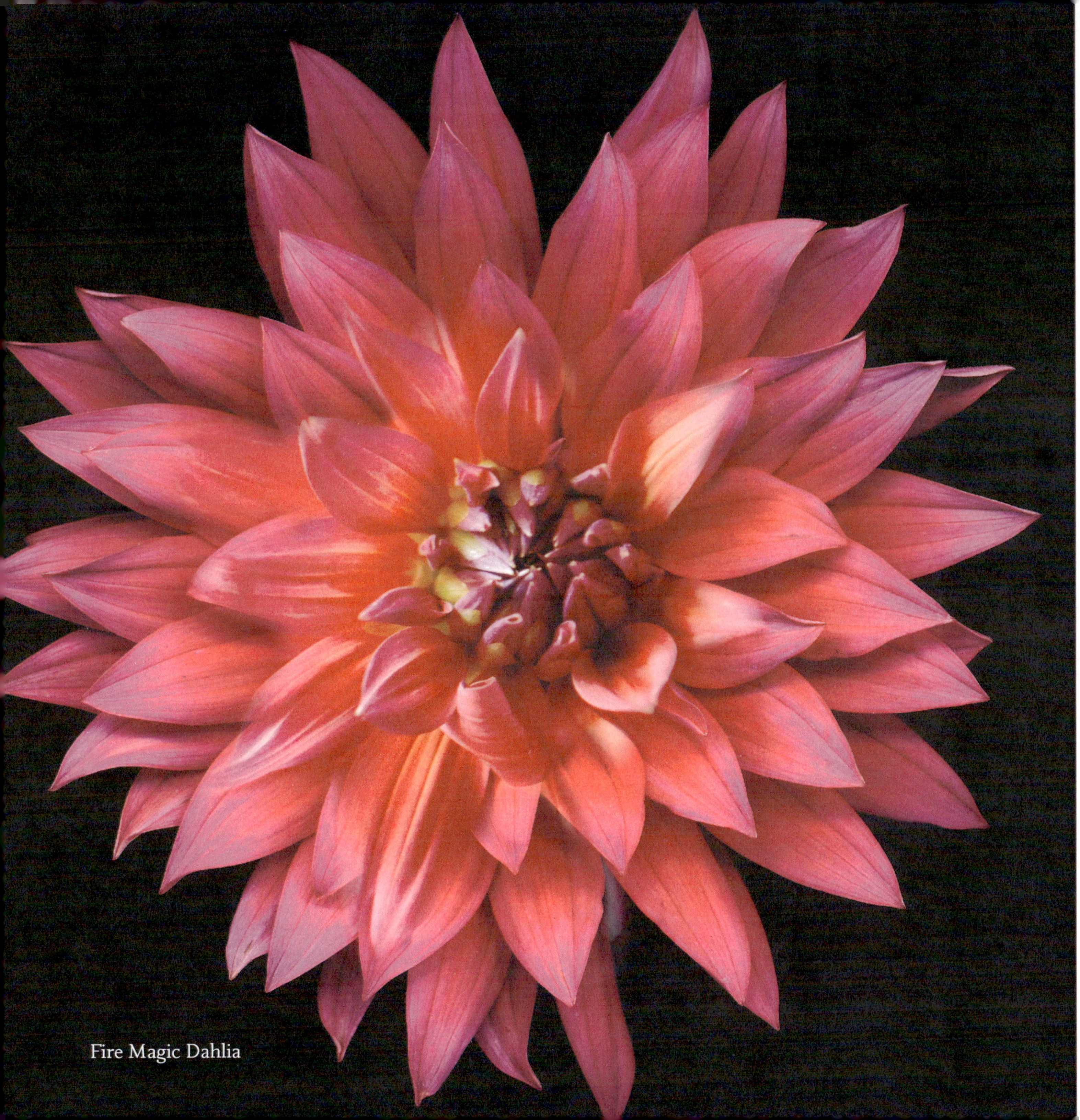
Fire Magic Dahlia

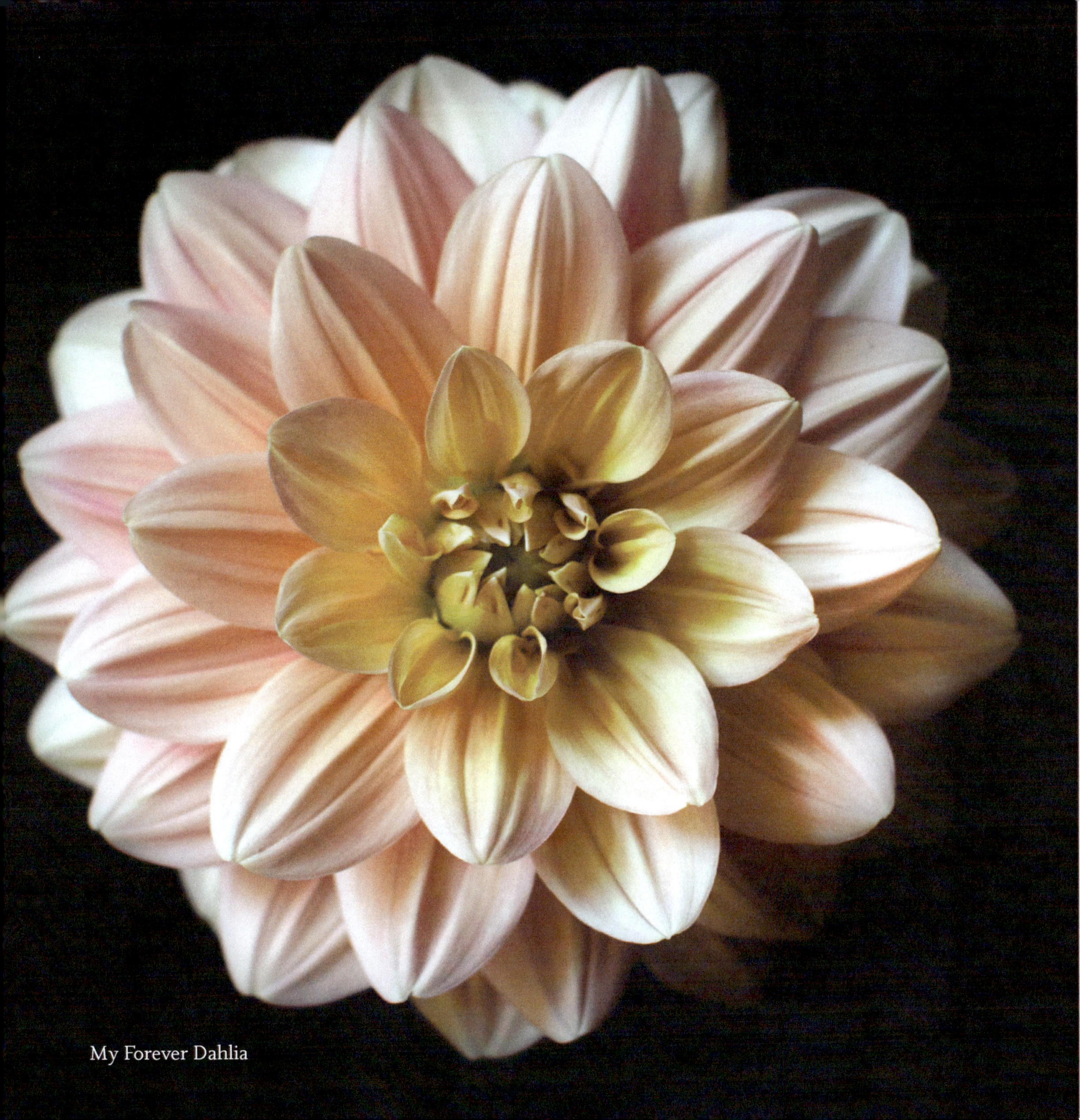
My Forever Dahlia

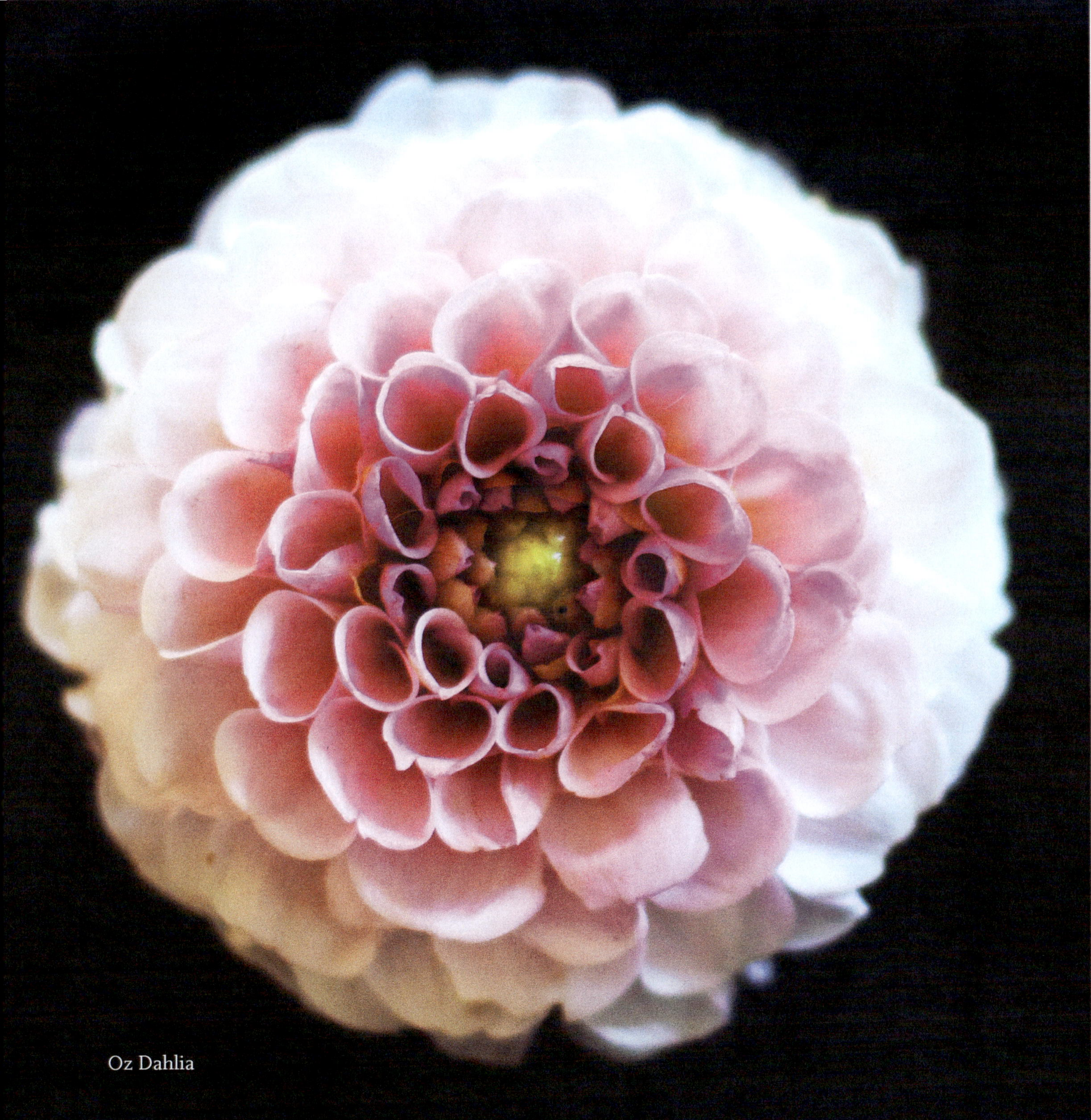

Oz Dahlia

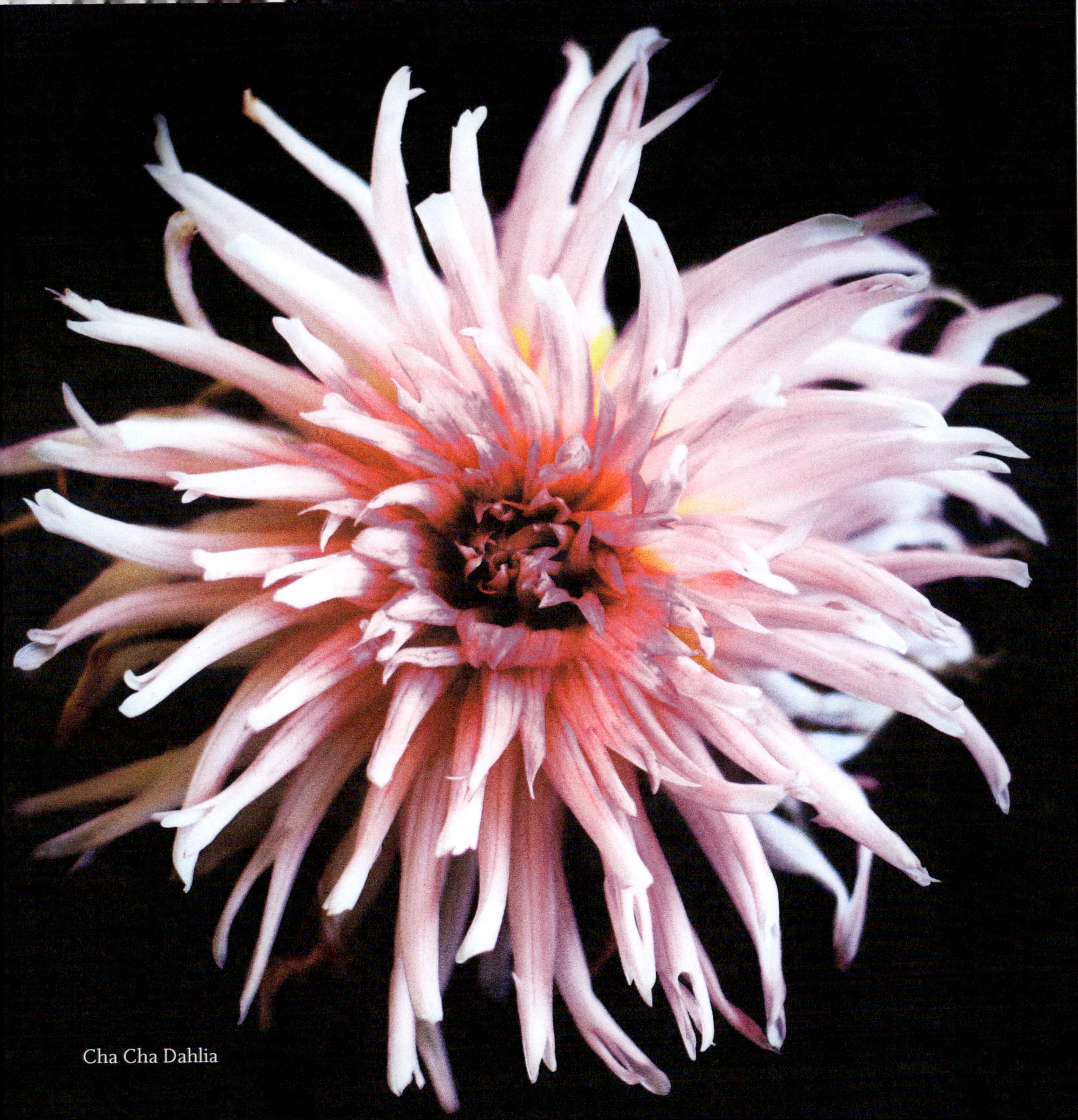
Cha Cha Dahlia

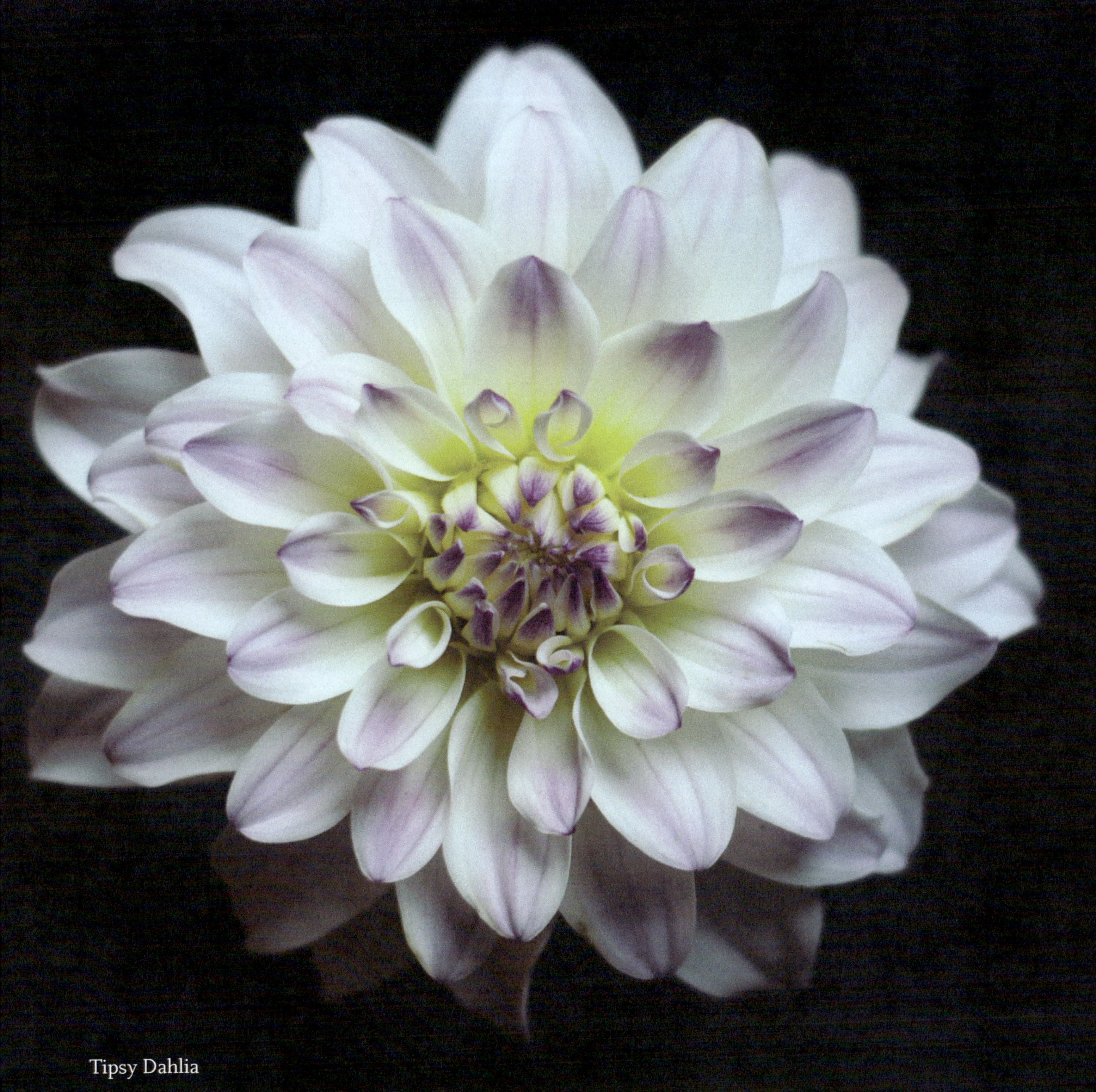

Tipsy Dahlia

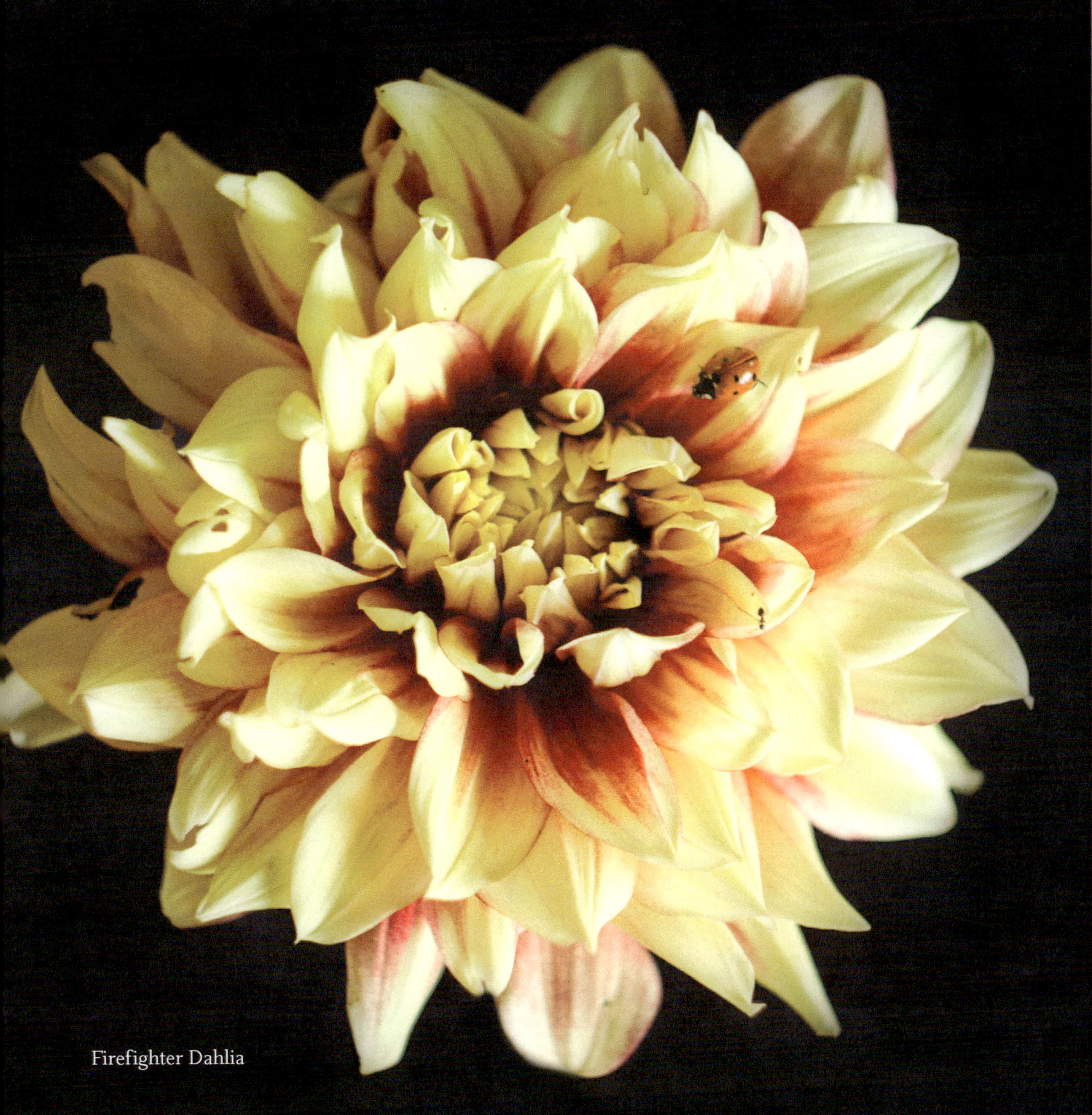

Firefighter Dahlia

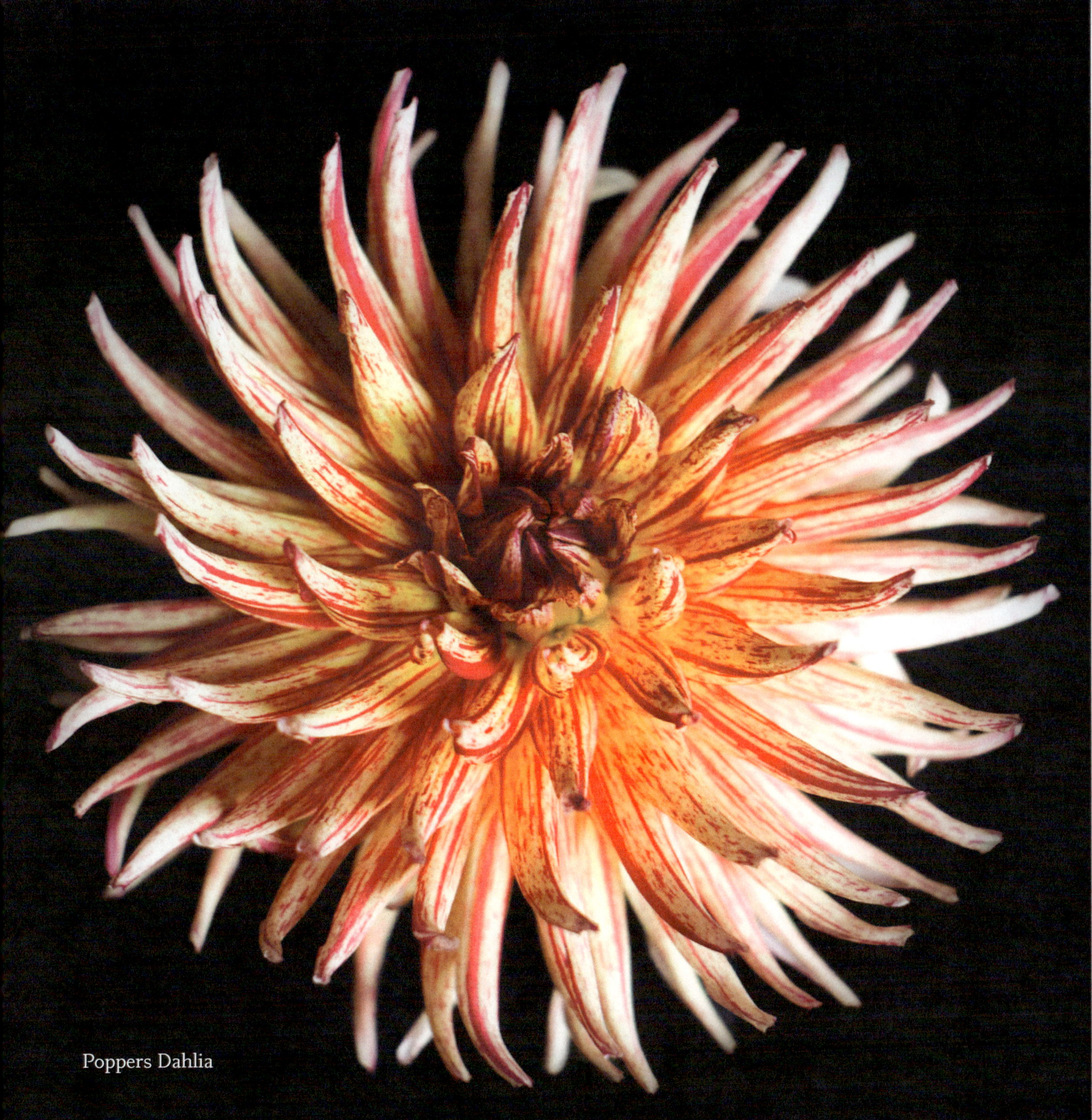

Poppers Dahlia

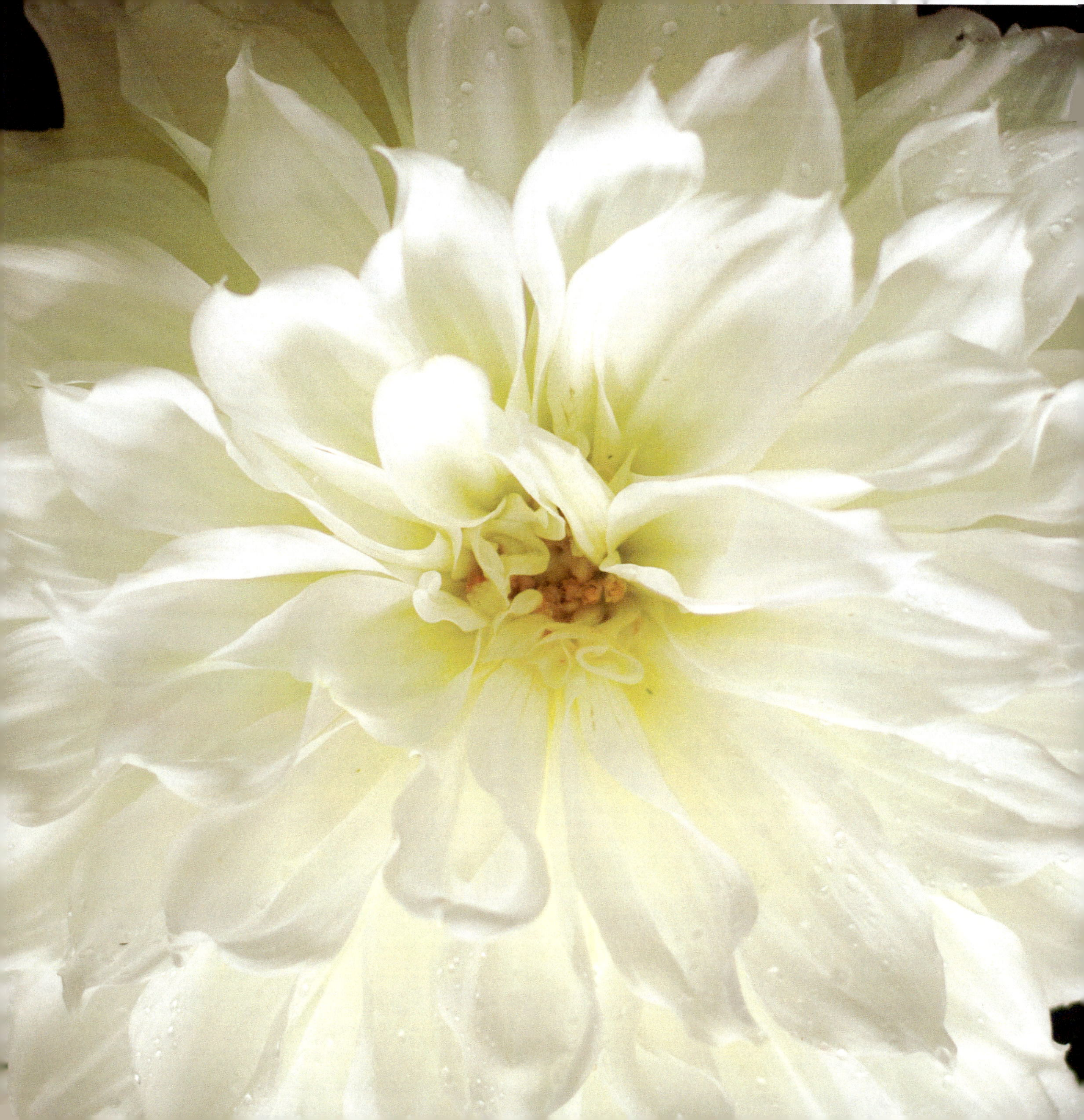

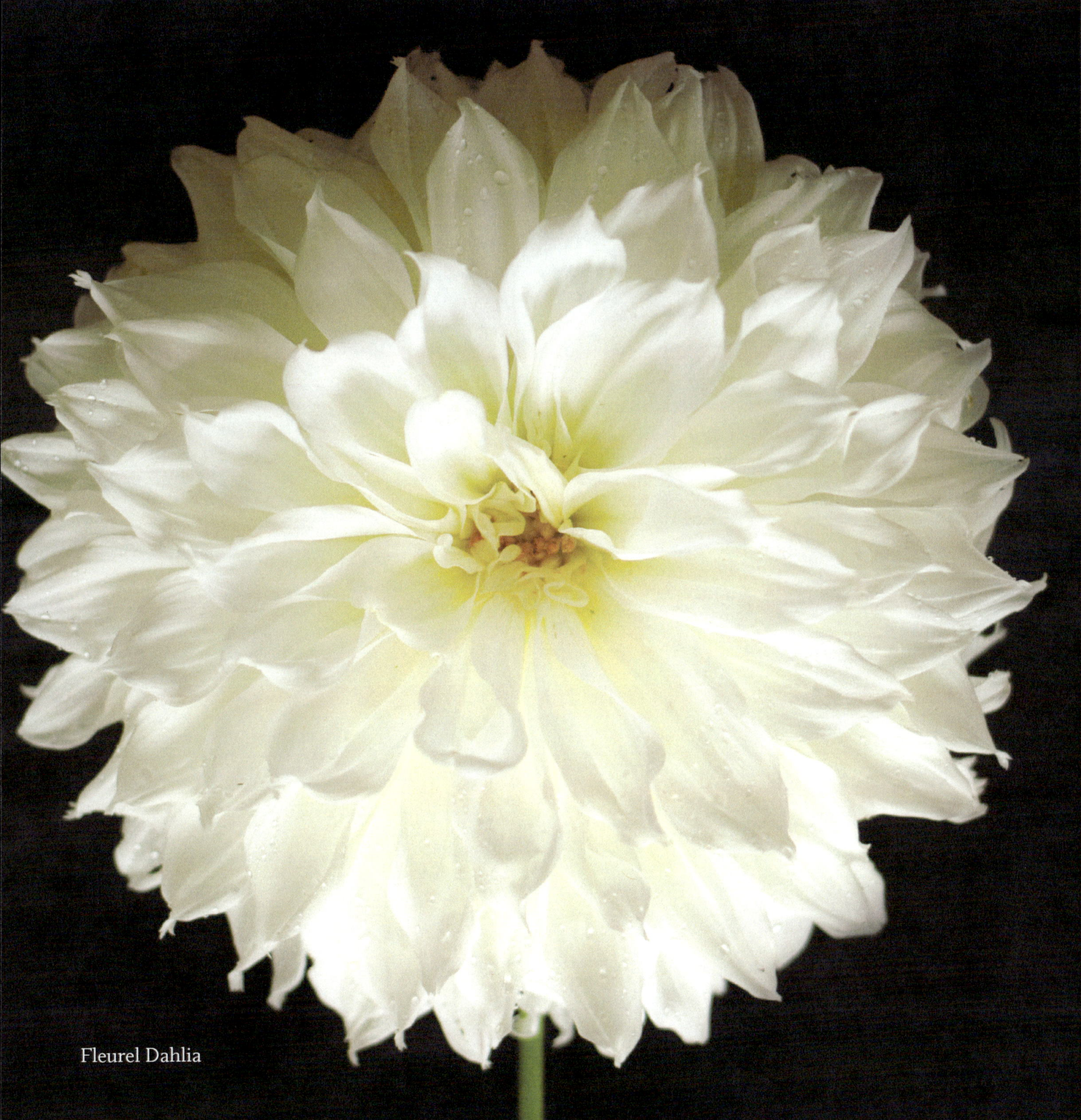
Fleurel Dahlia

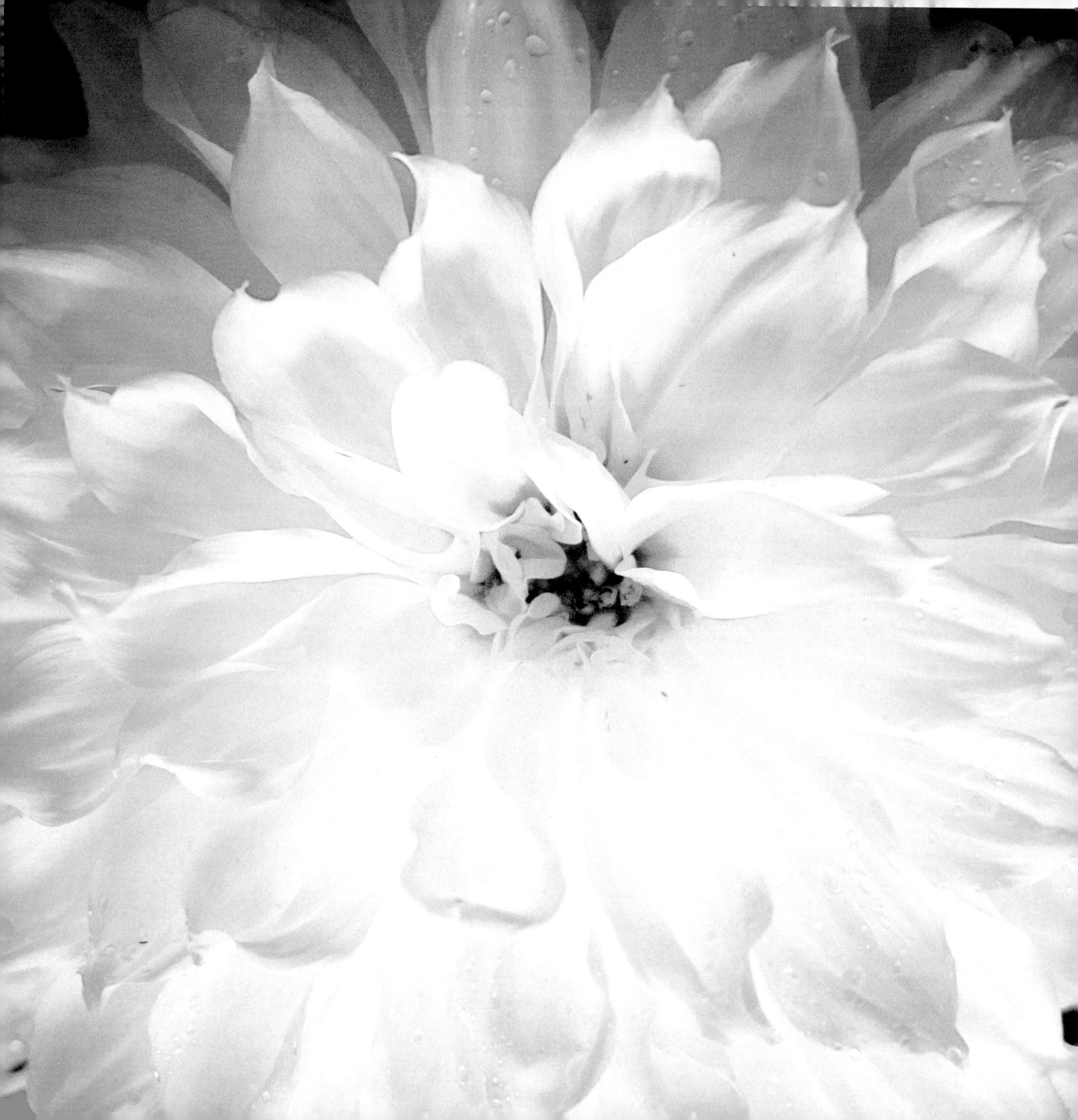

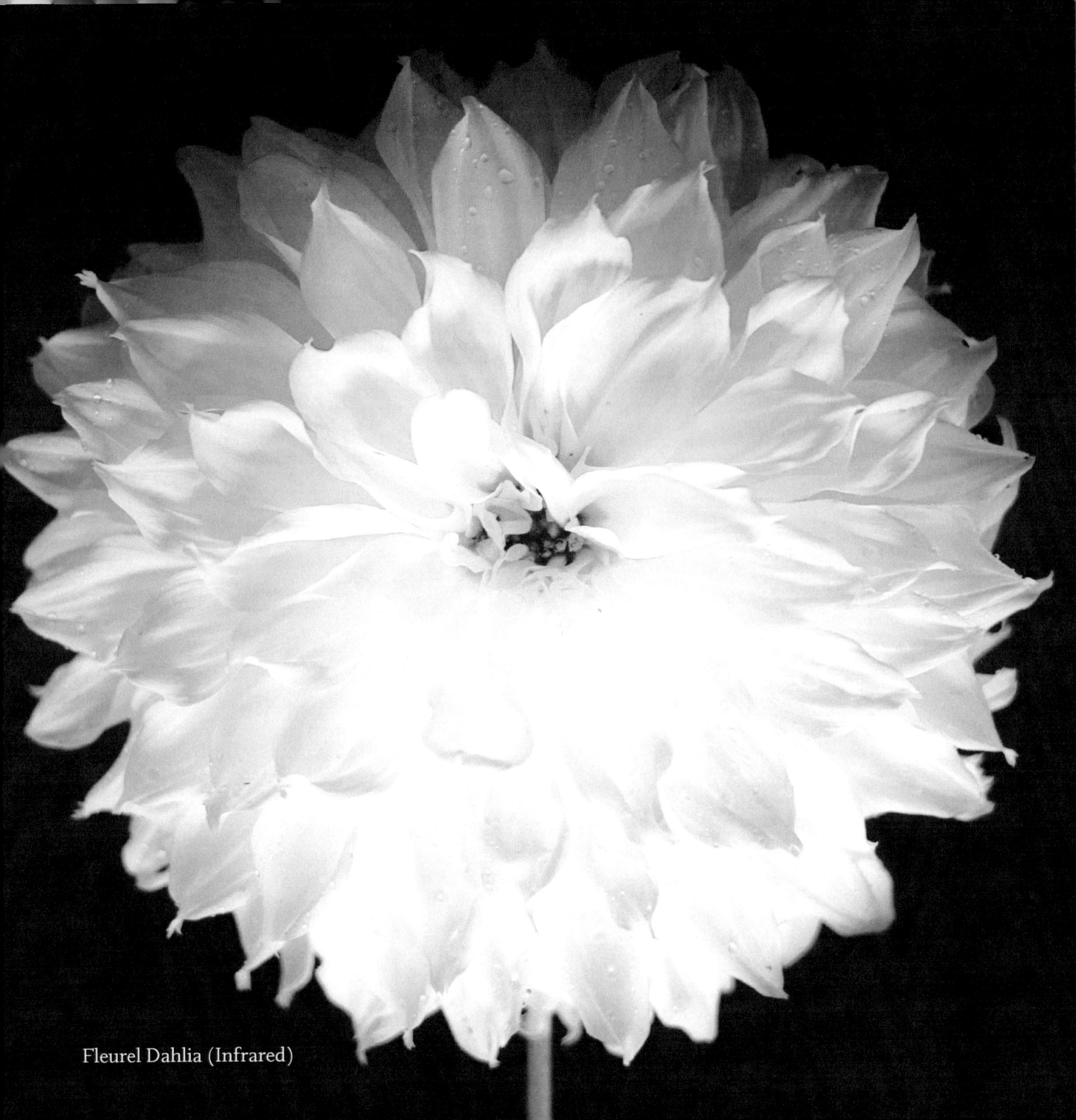

Fleurel Dahlia (Infrared)

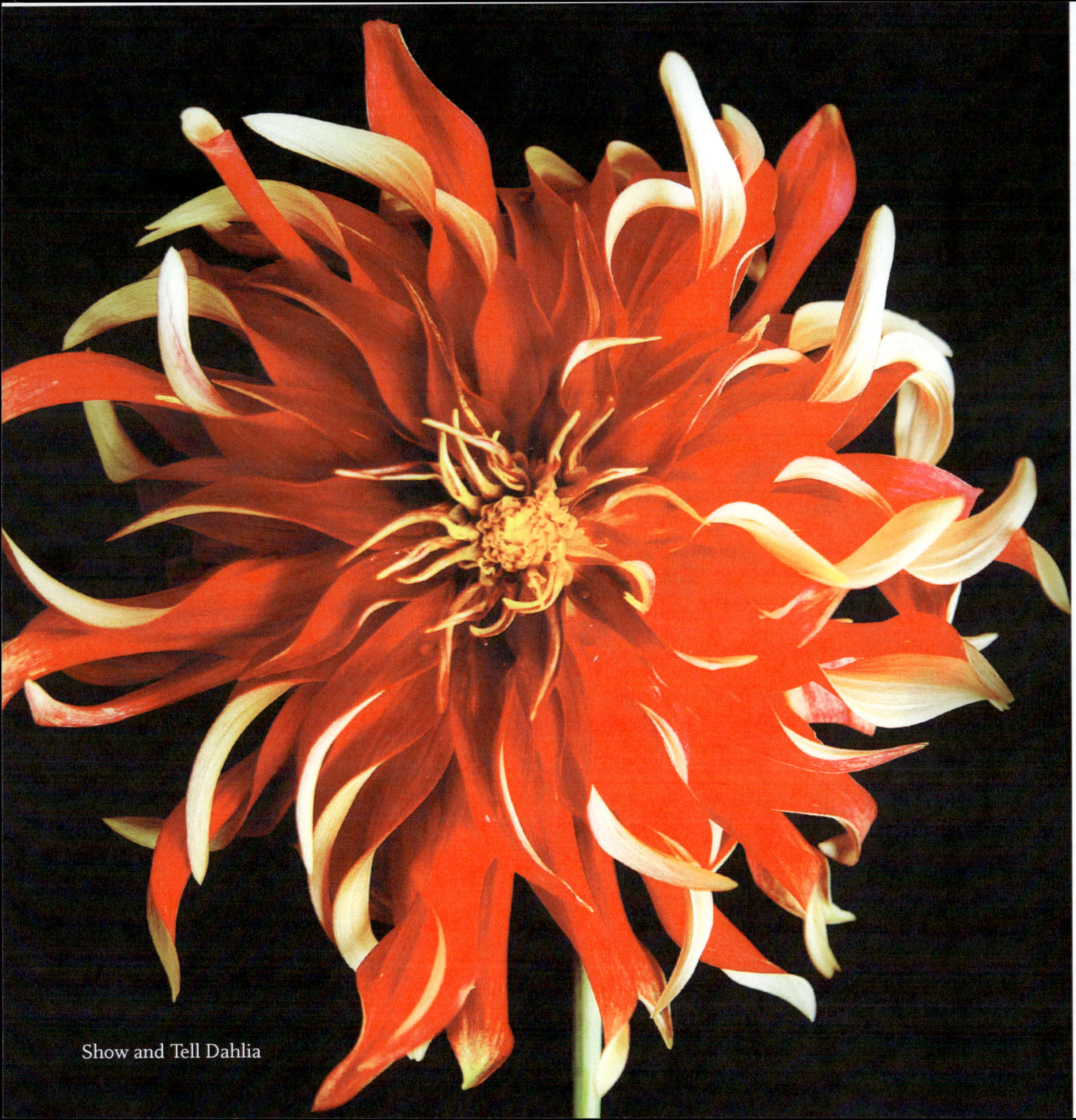
Show and Tell Dahlia

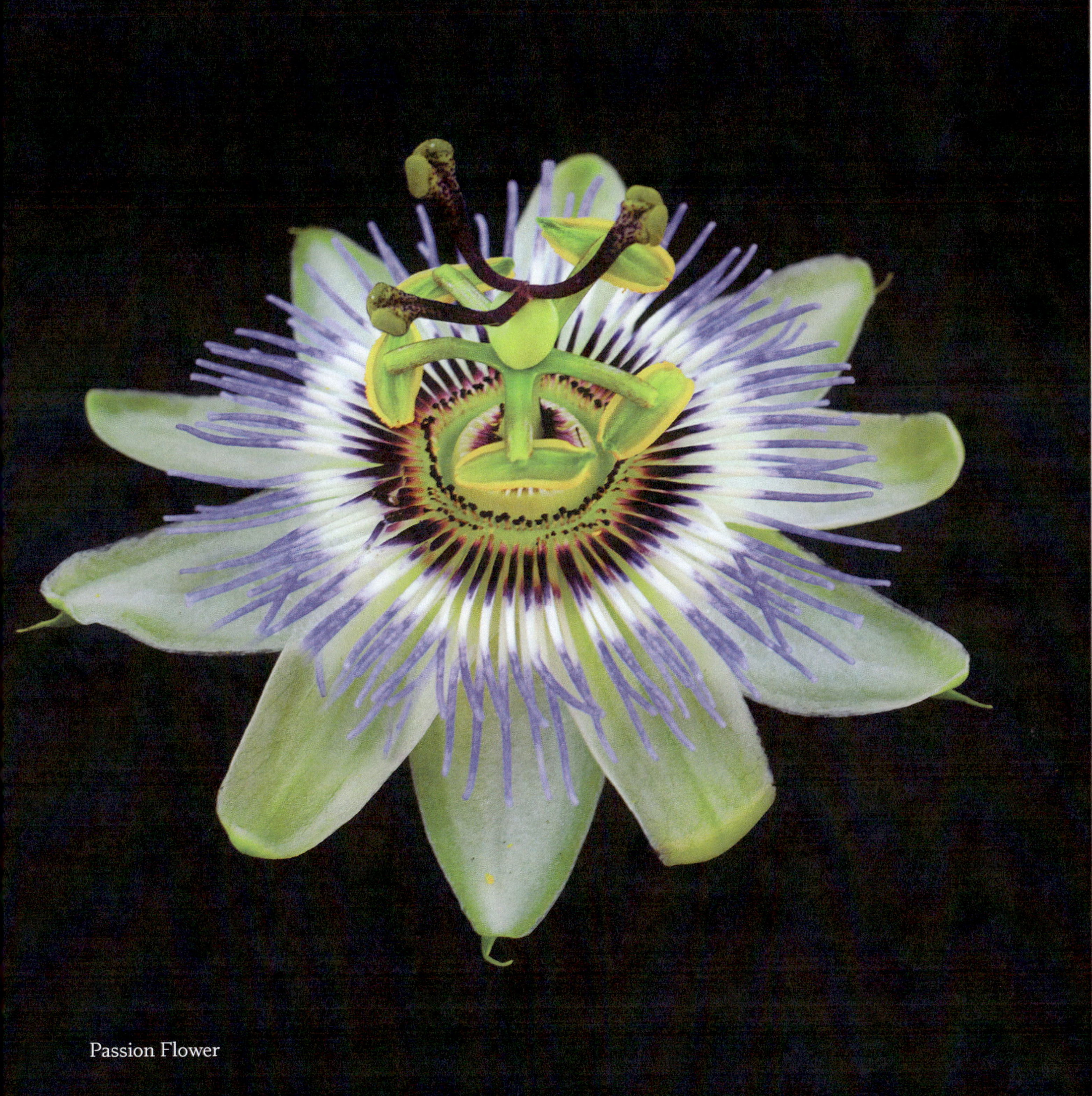
Passion Flower

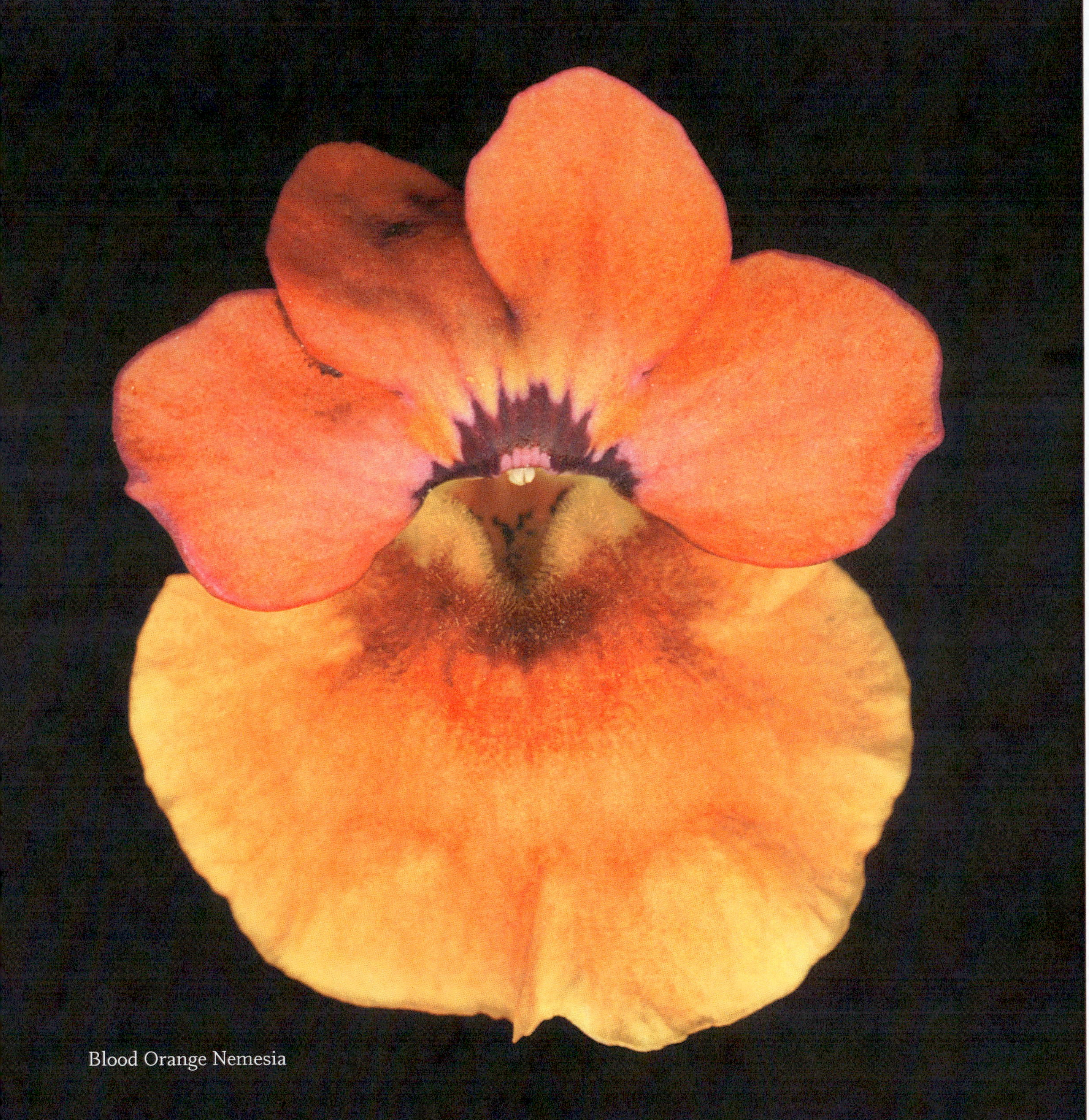
Blood Orange Nemesia

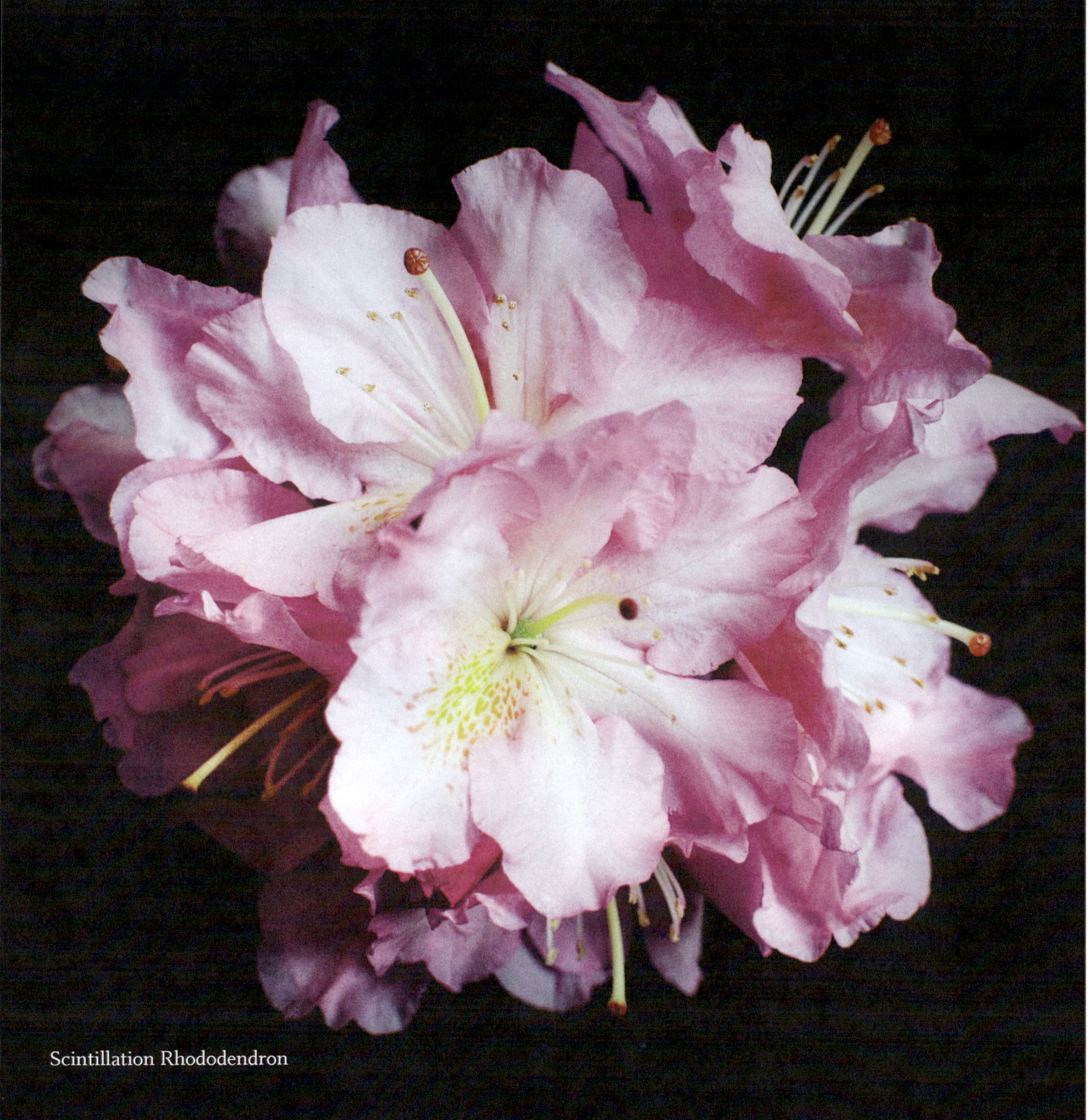

Scintillation Rhododendron

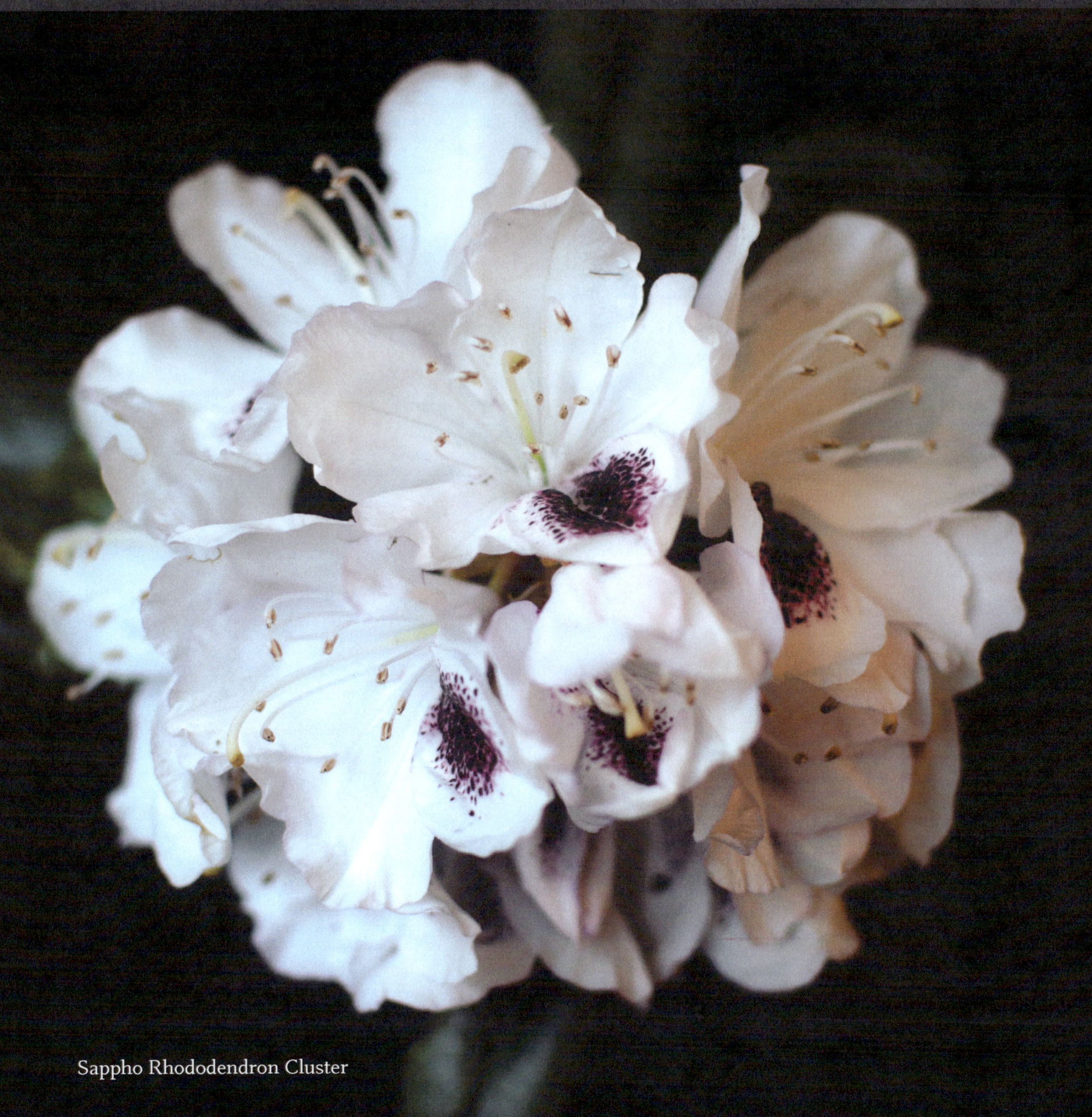

Sappho Rhododendron Cluster

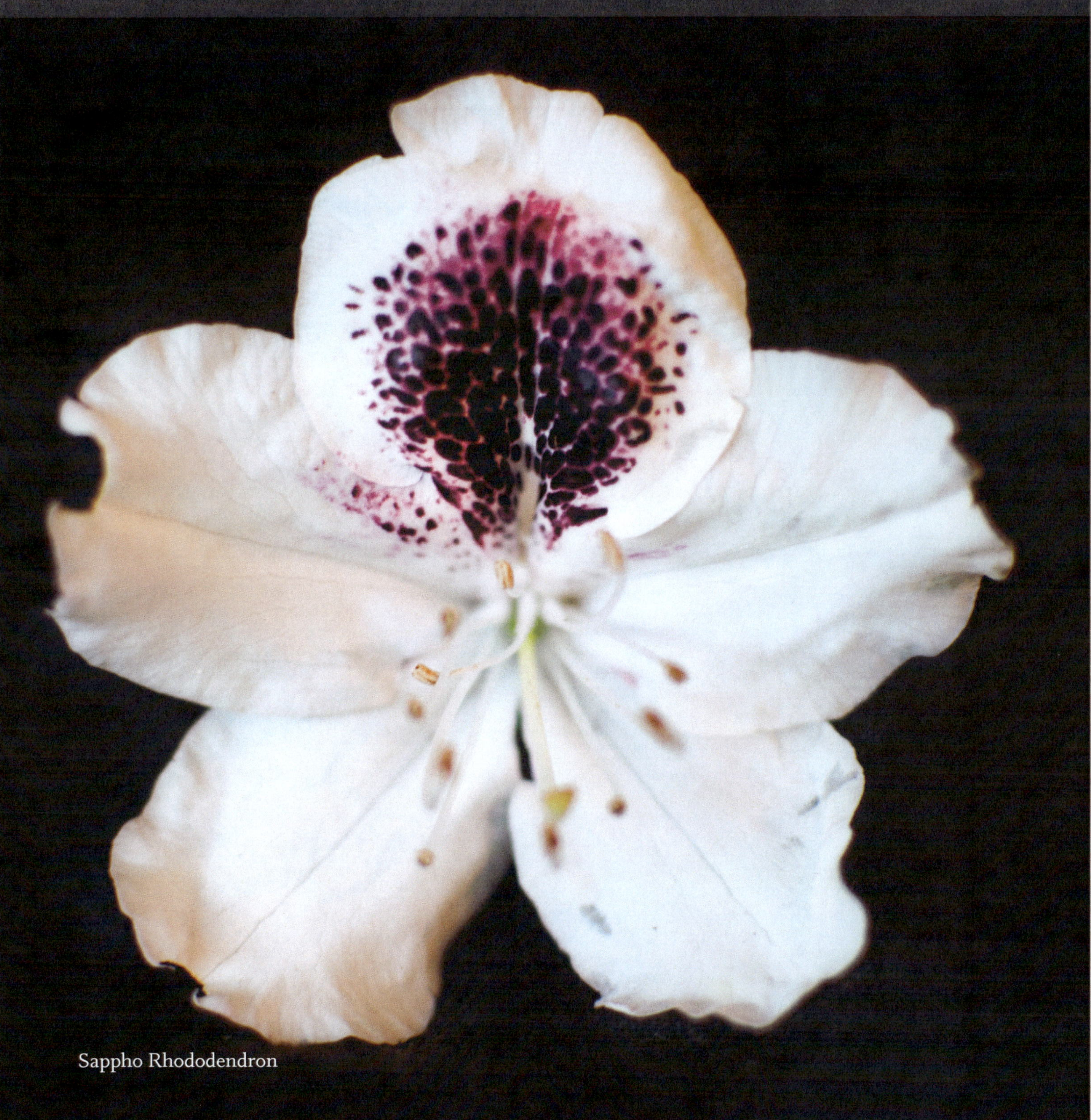

Sappho Rhododendron

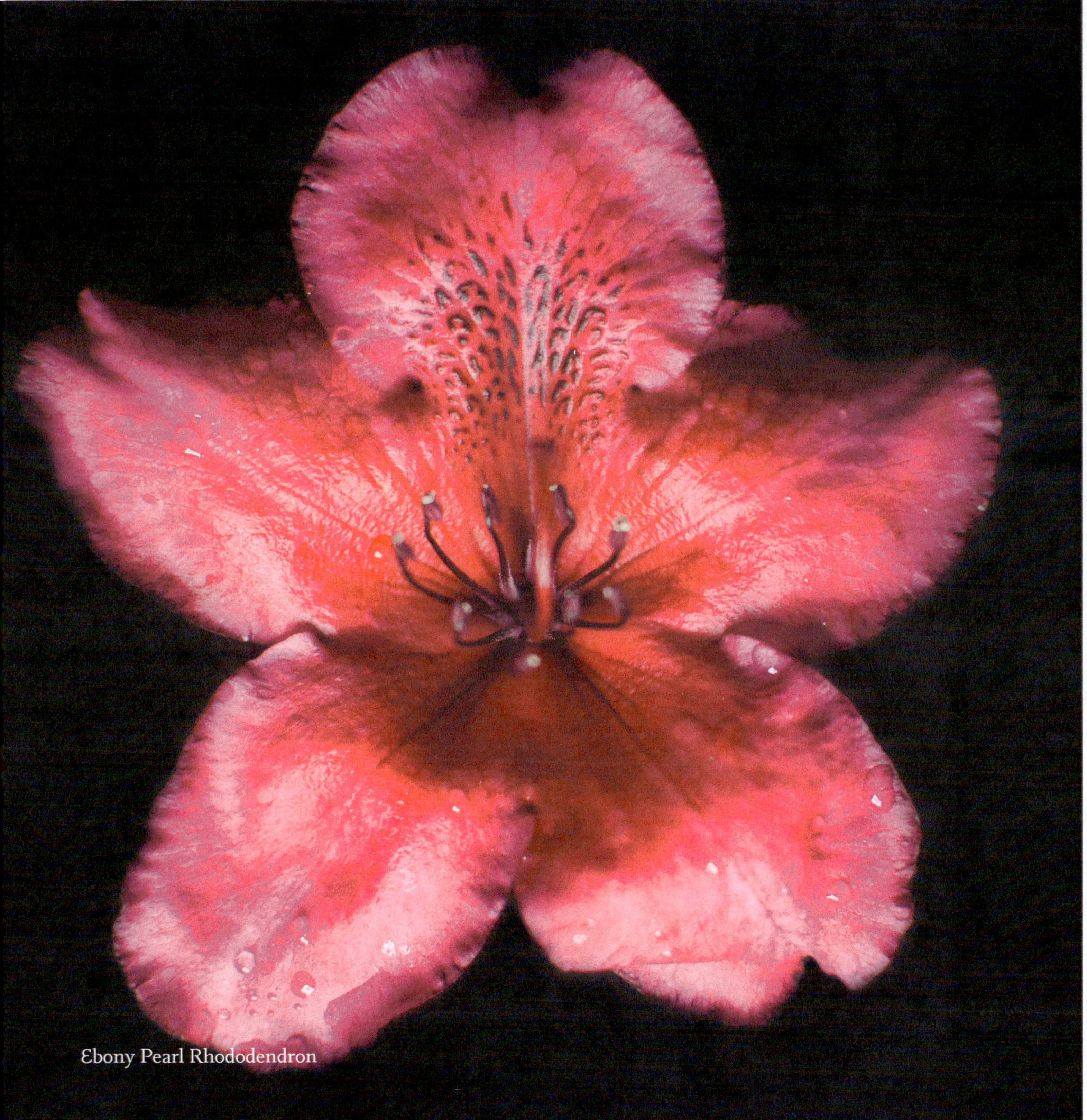

Ebony Pearl Rhododendron

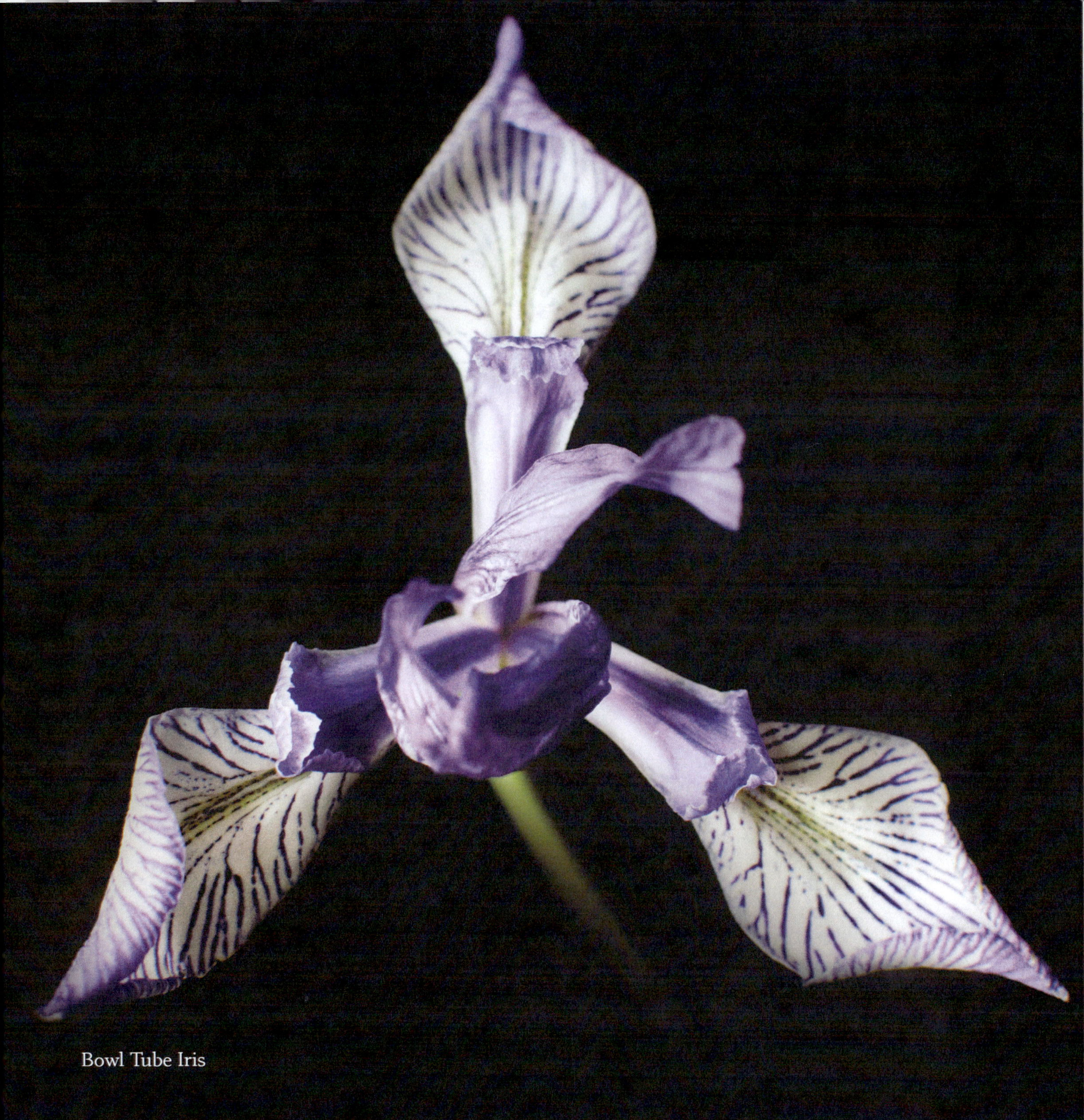

Bowl Tube Iris

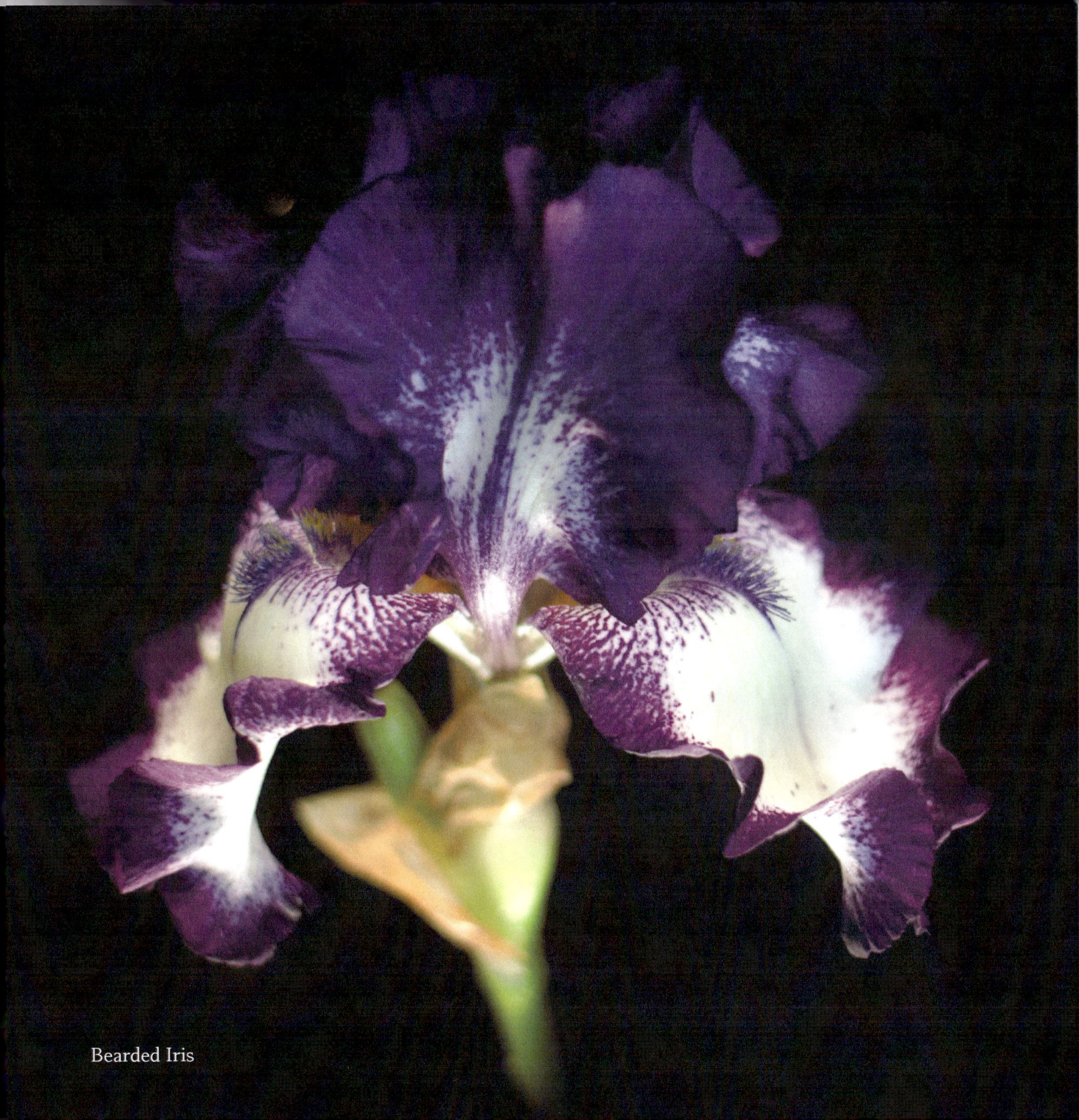

Bearded Iris

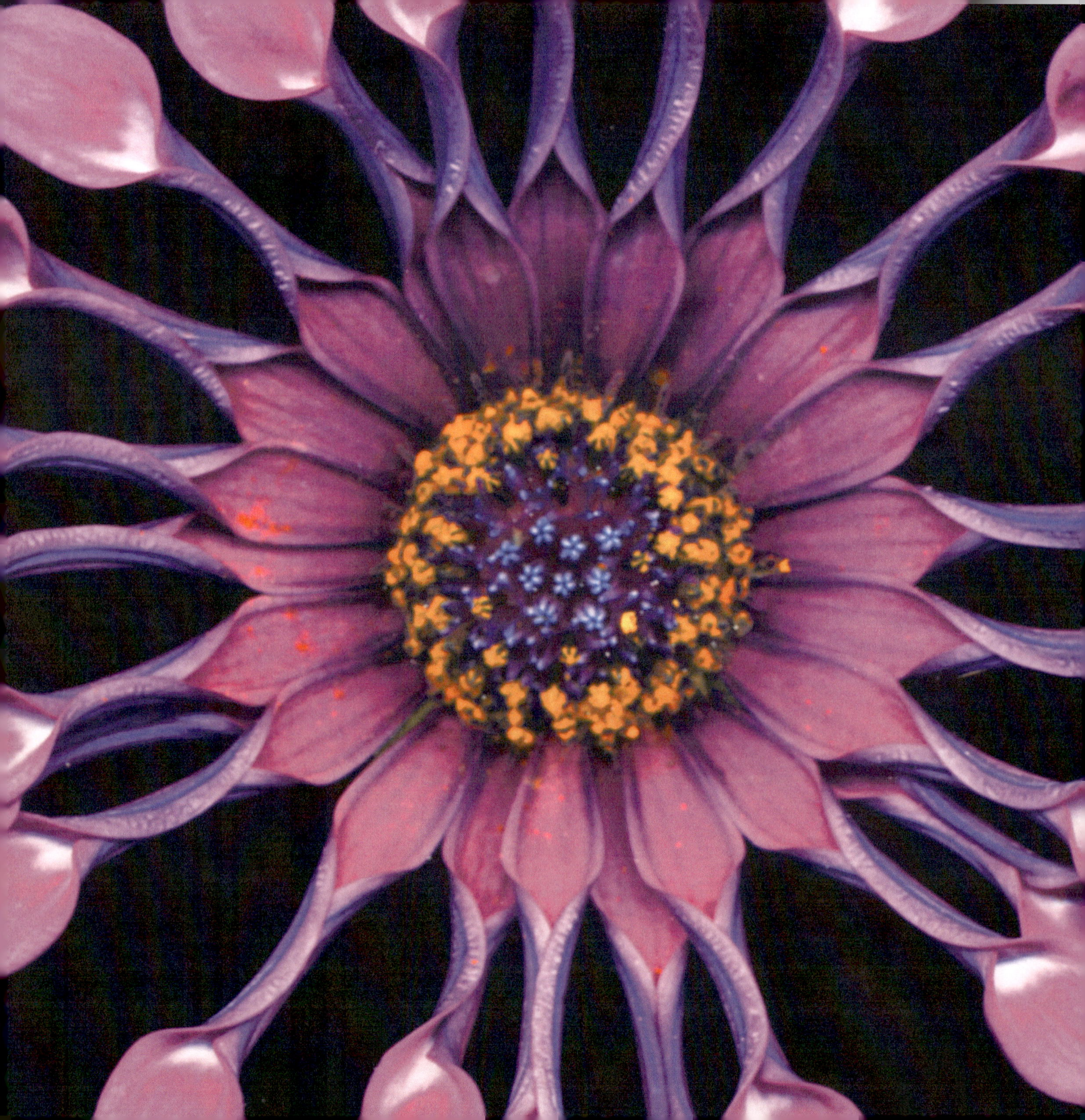

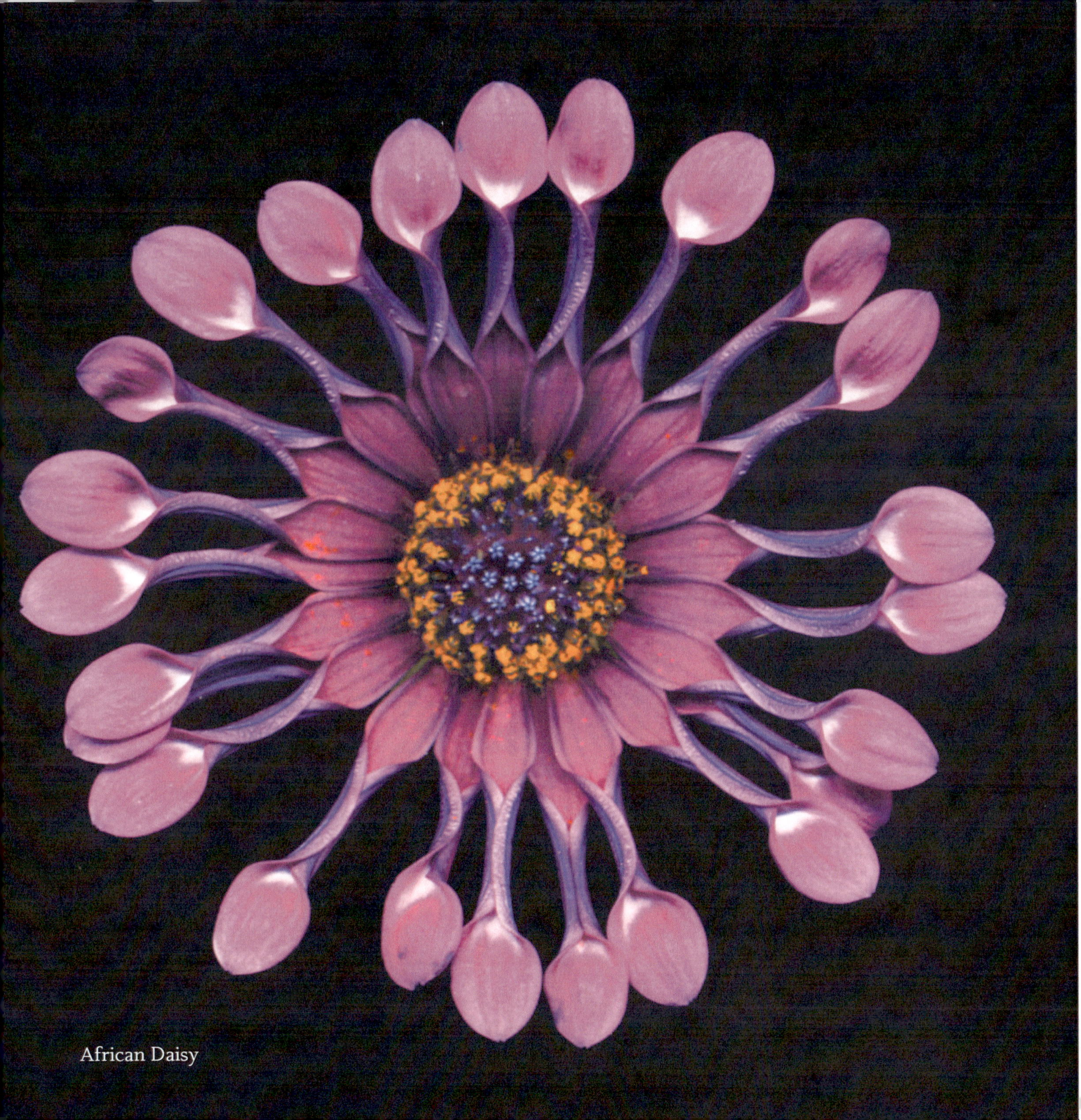

African Daisy

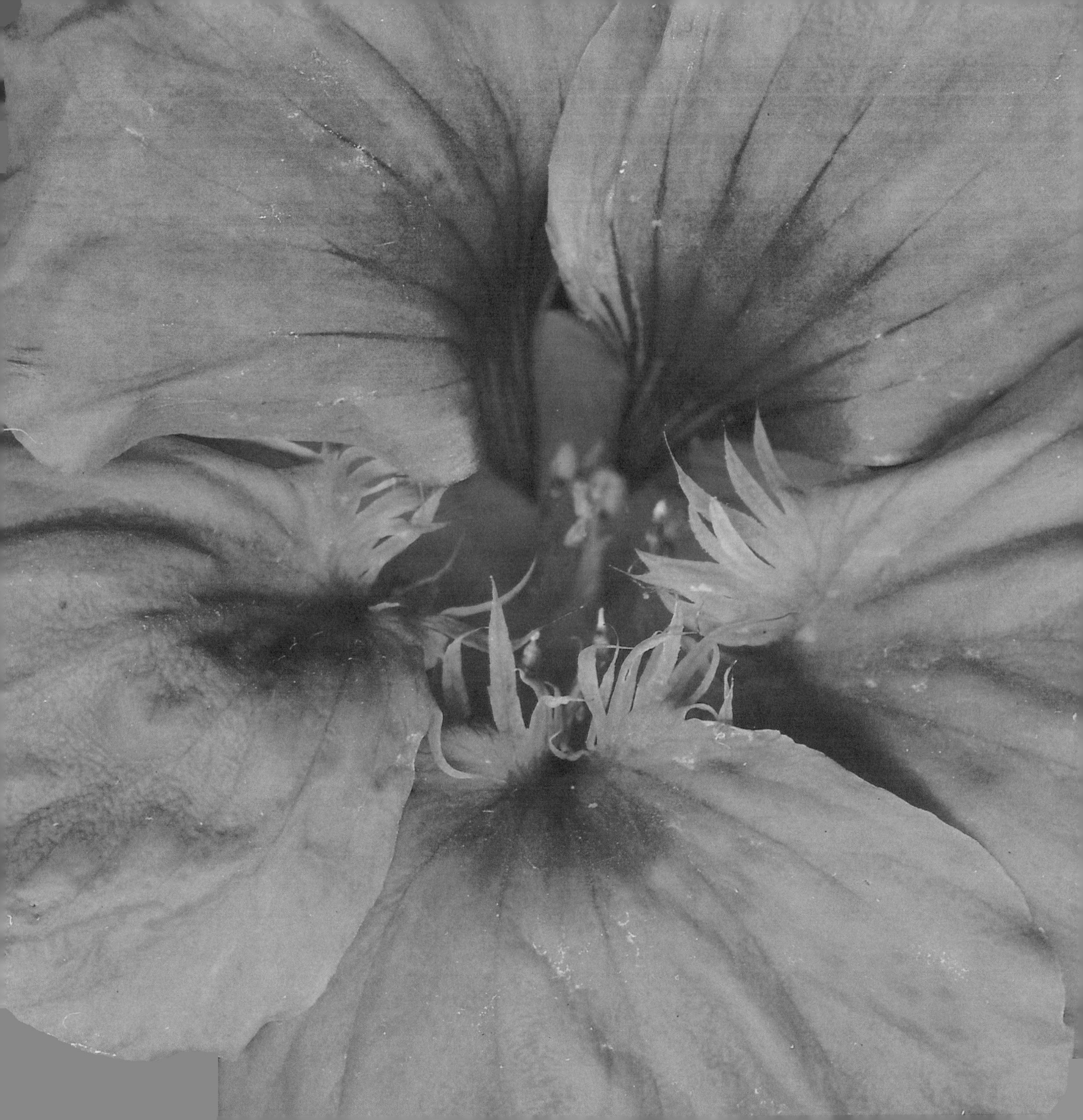

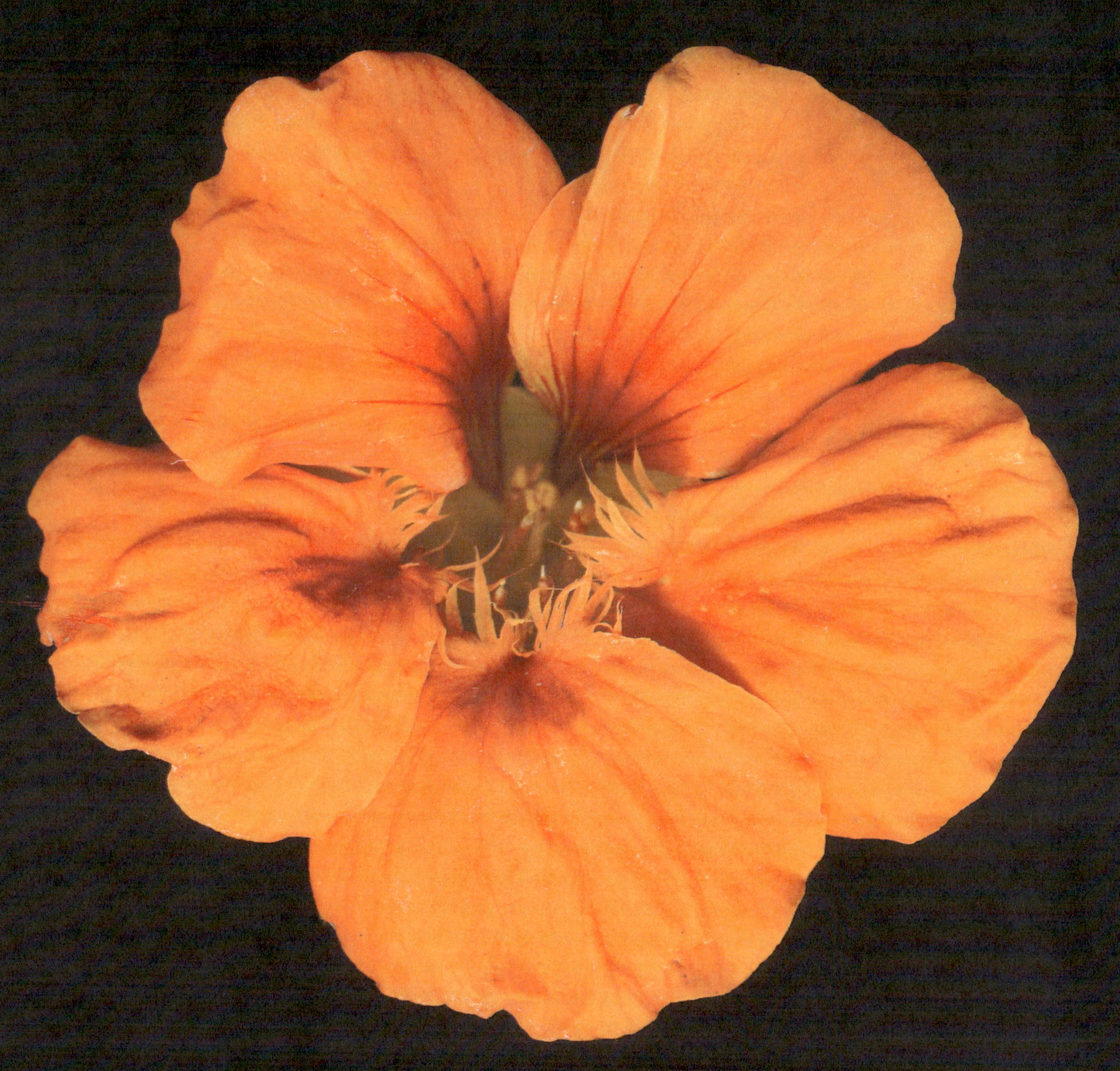

Nasturtium

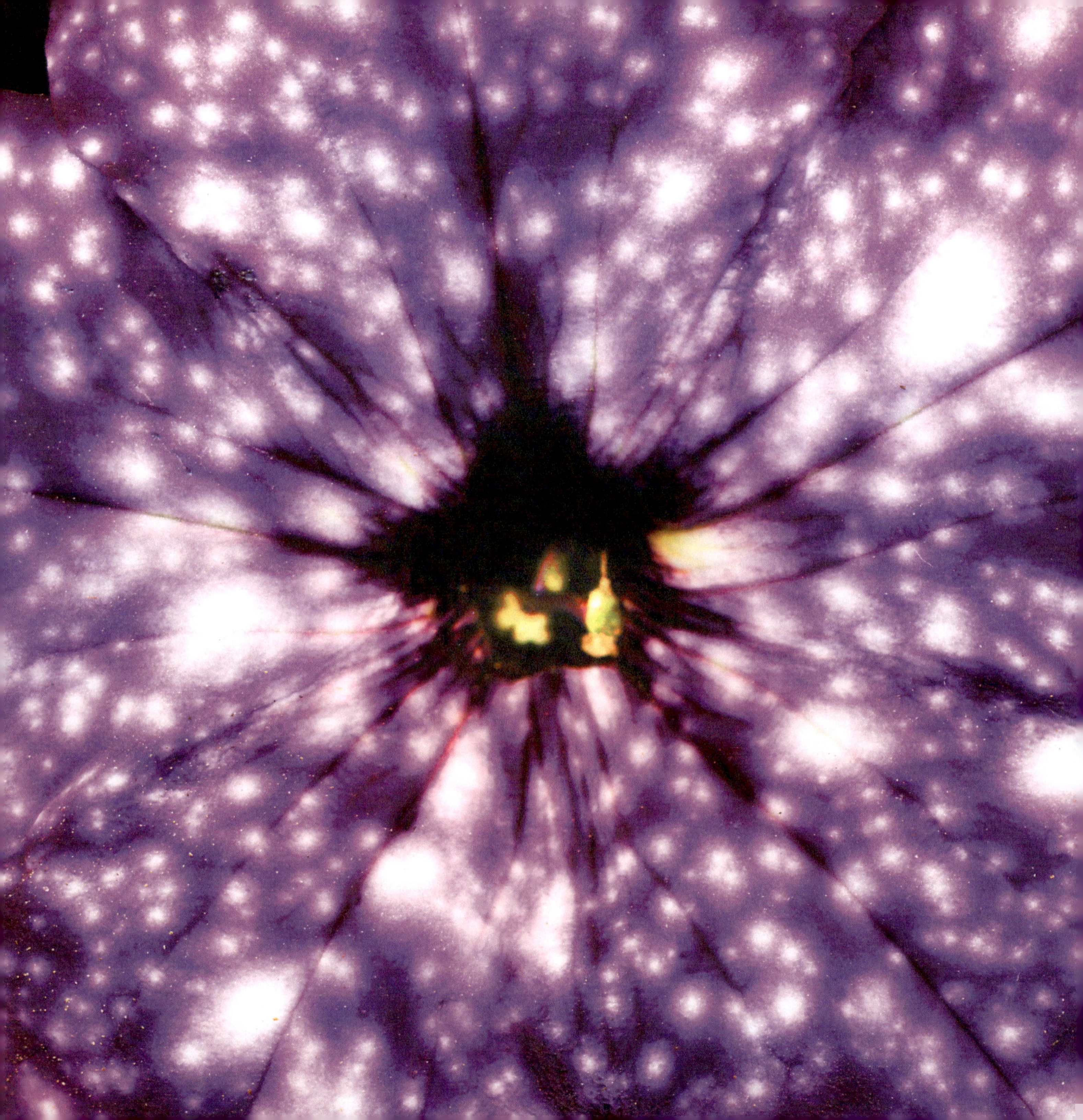

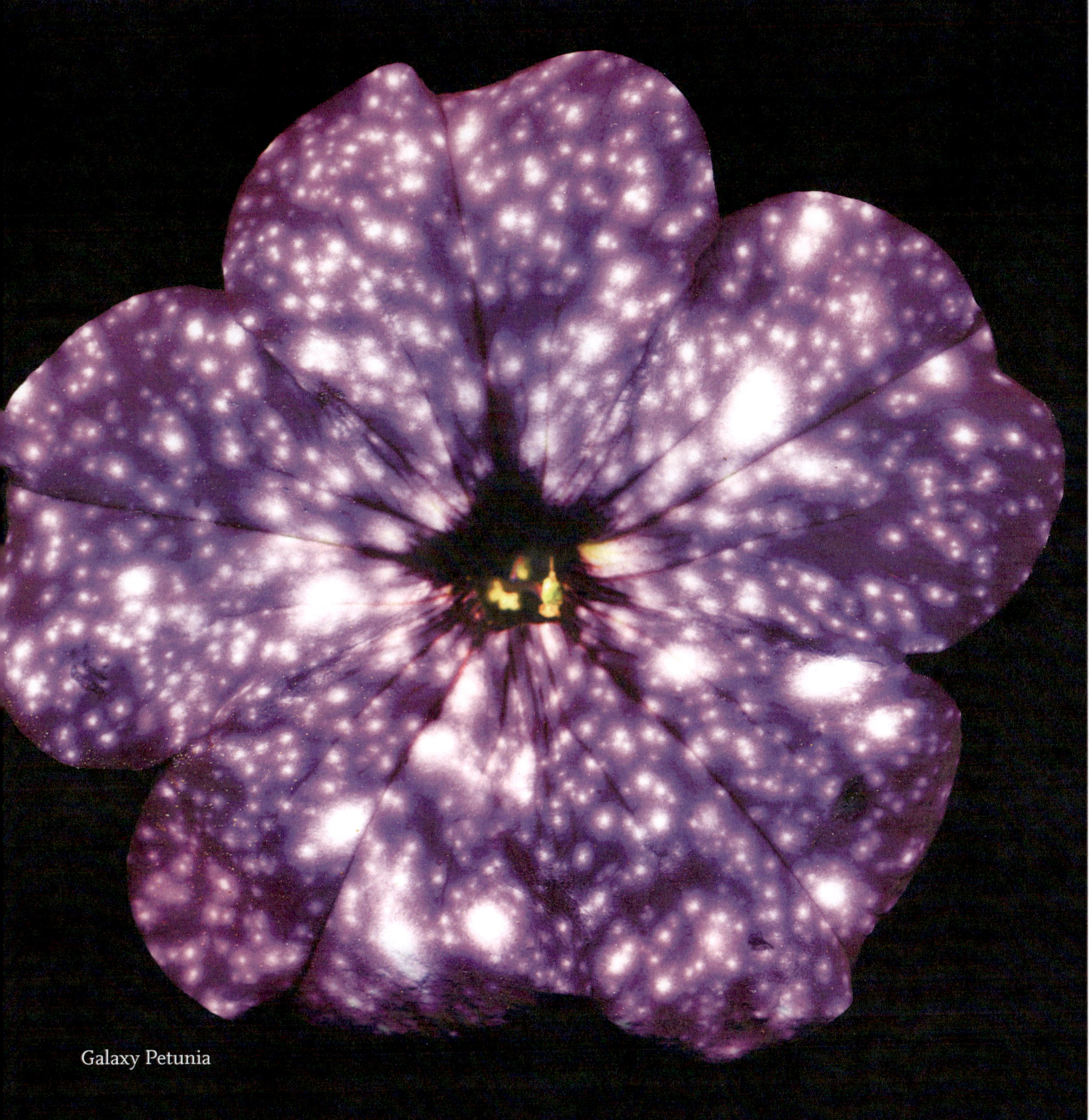

Galaxy Petunia

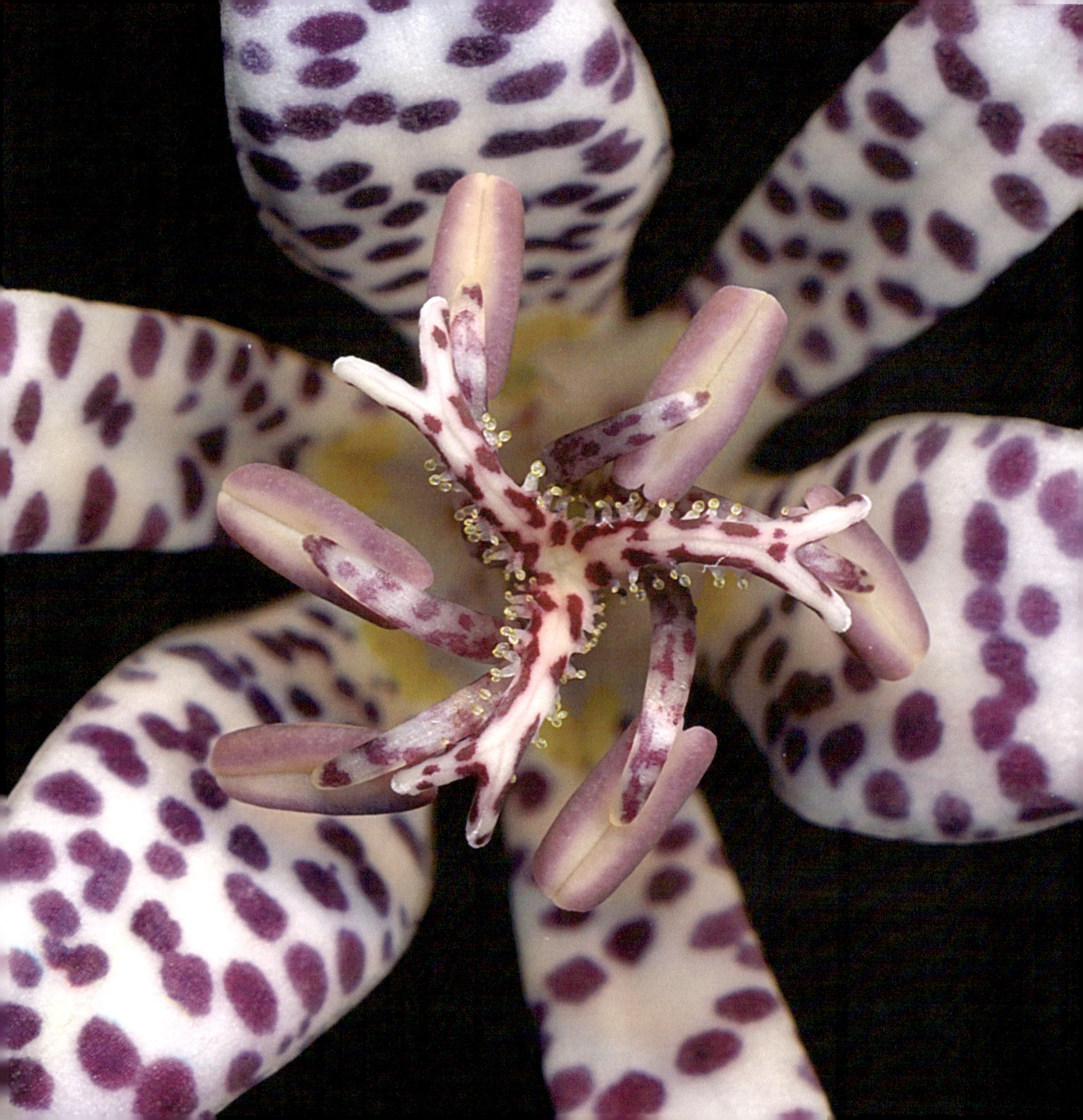

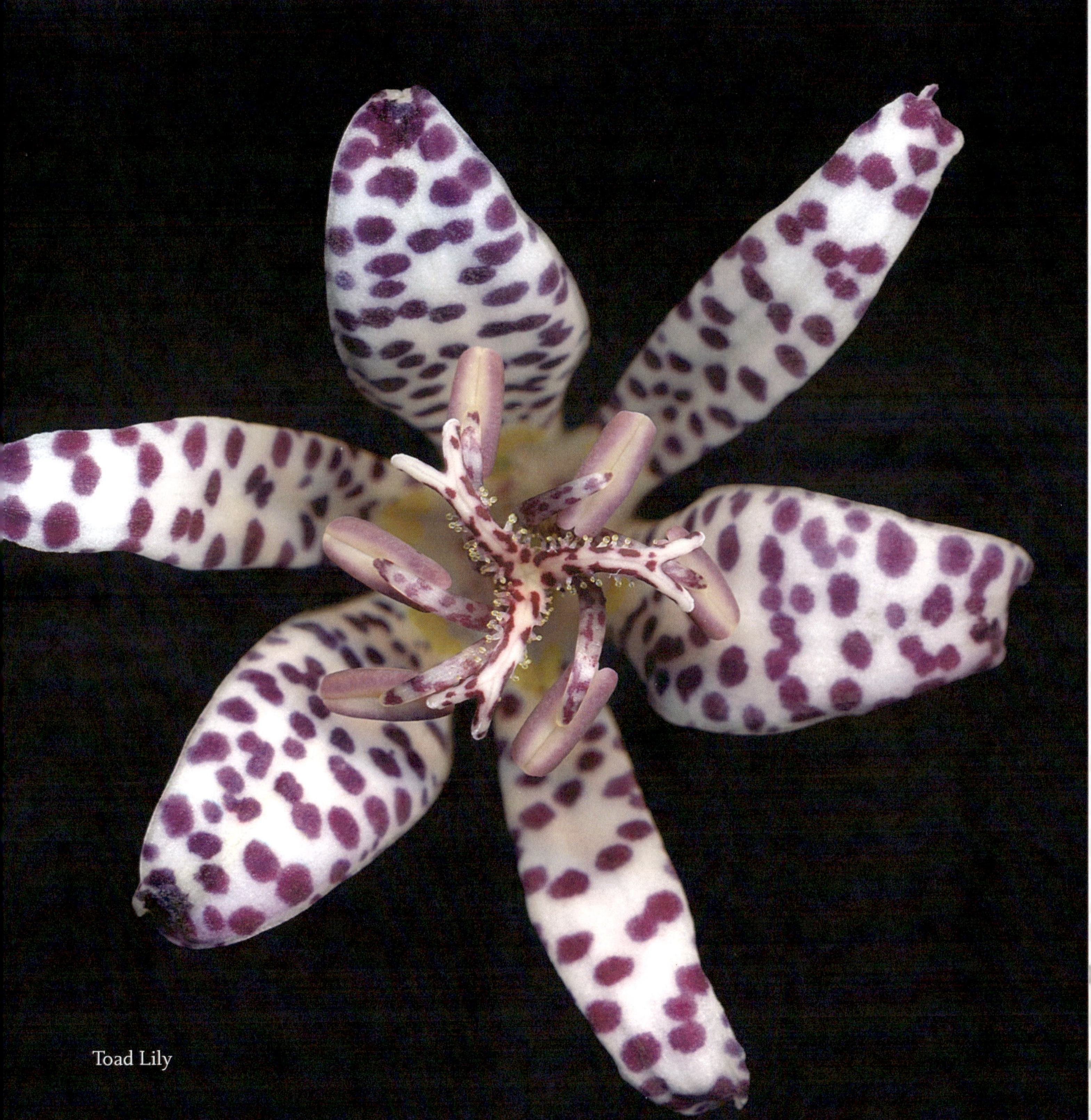

Toad Lily

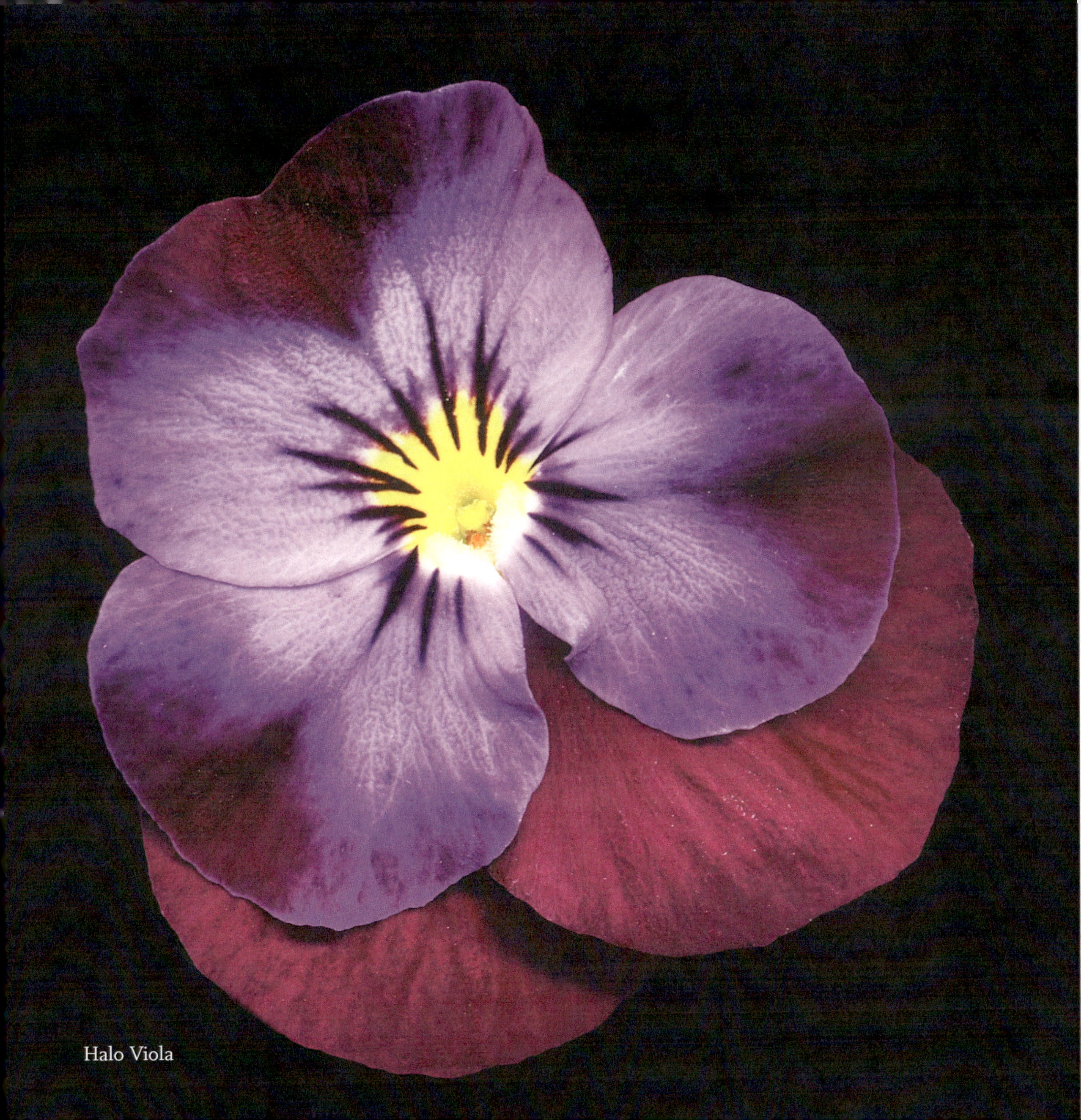
Halo Viola

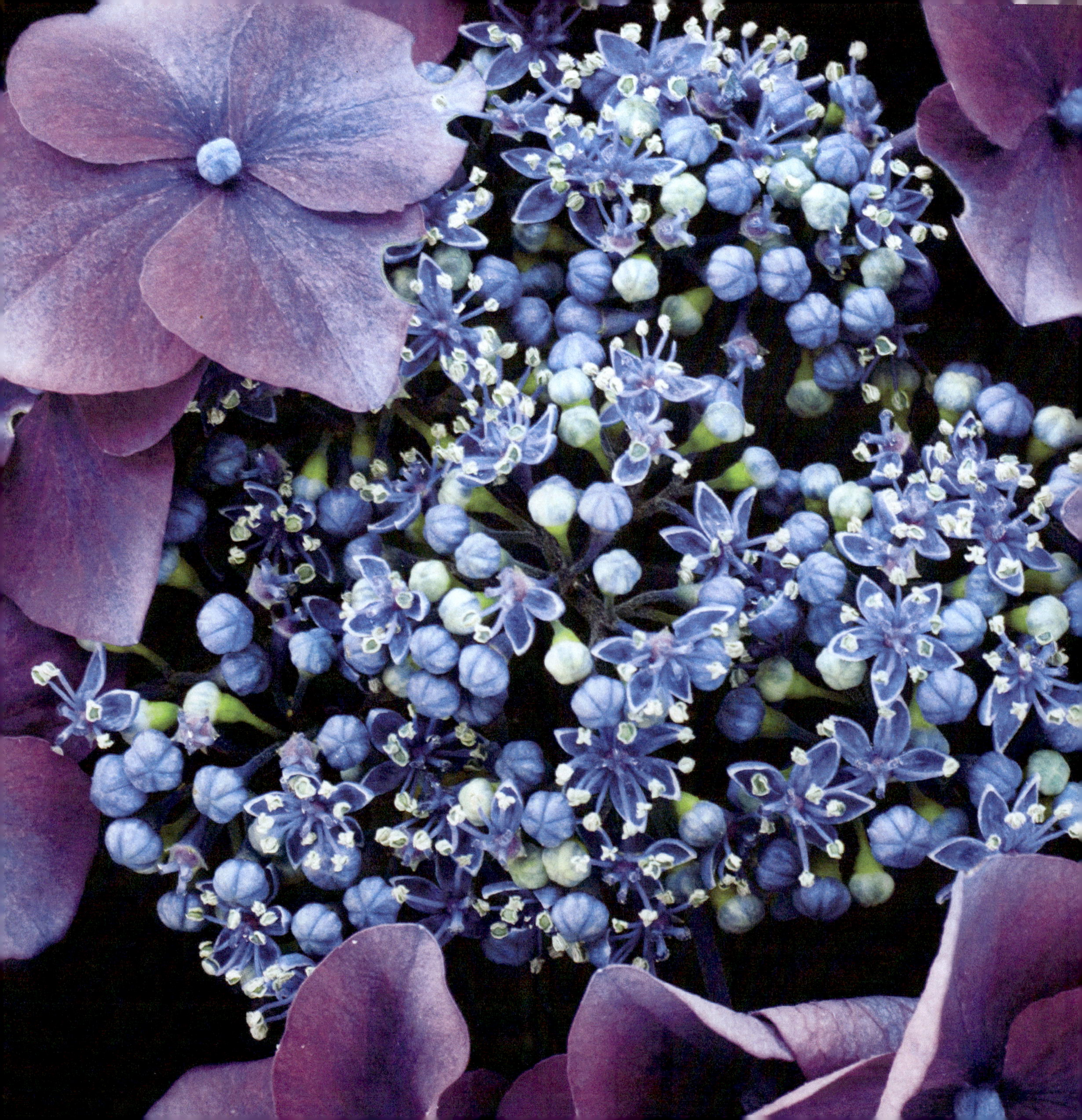

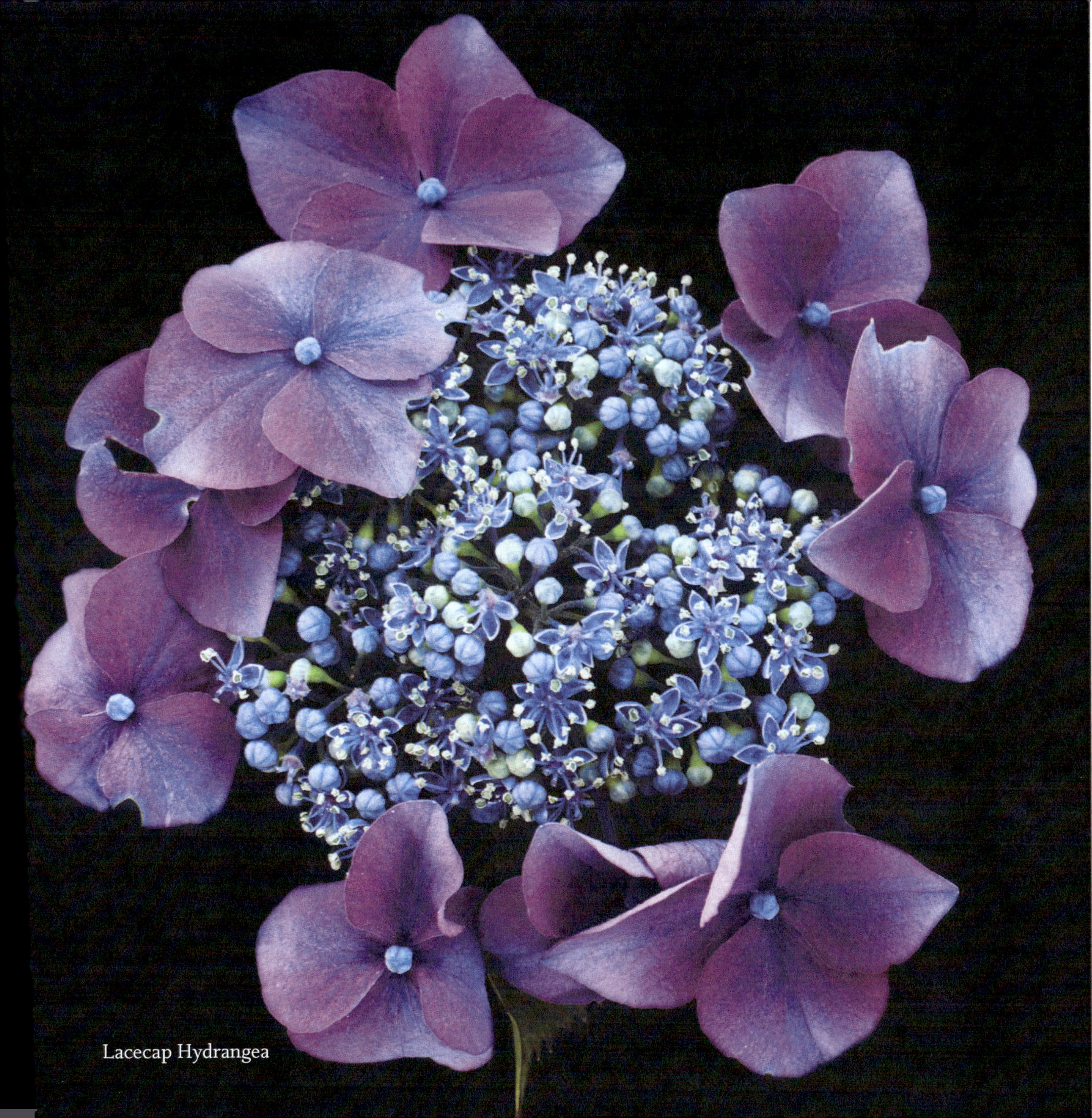

Lacecap Hydrangea

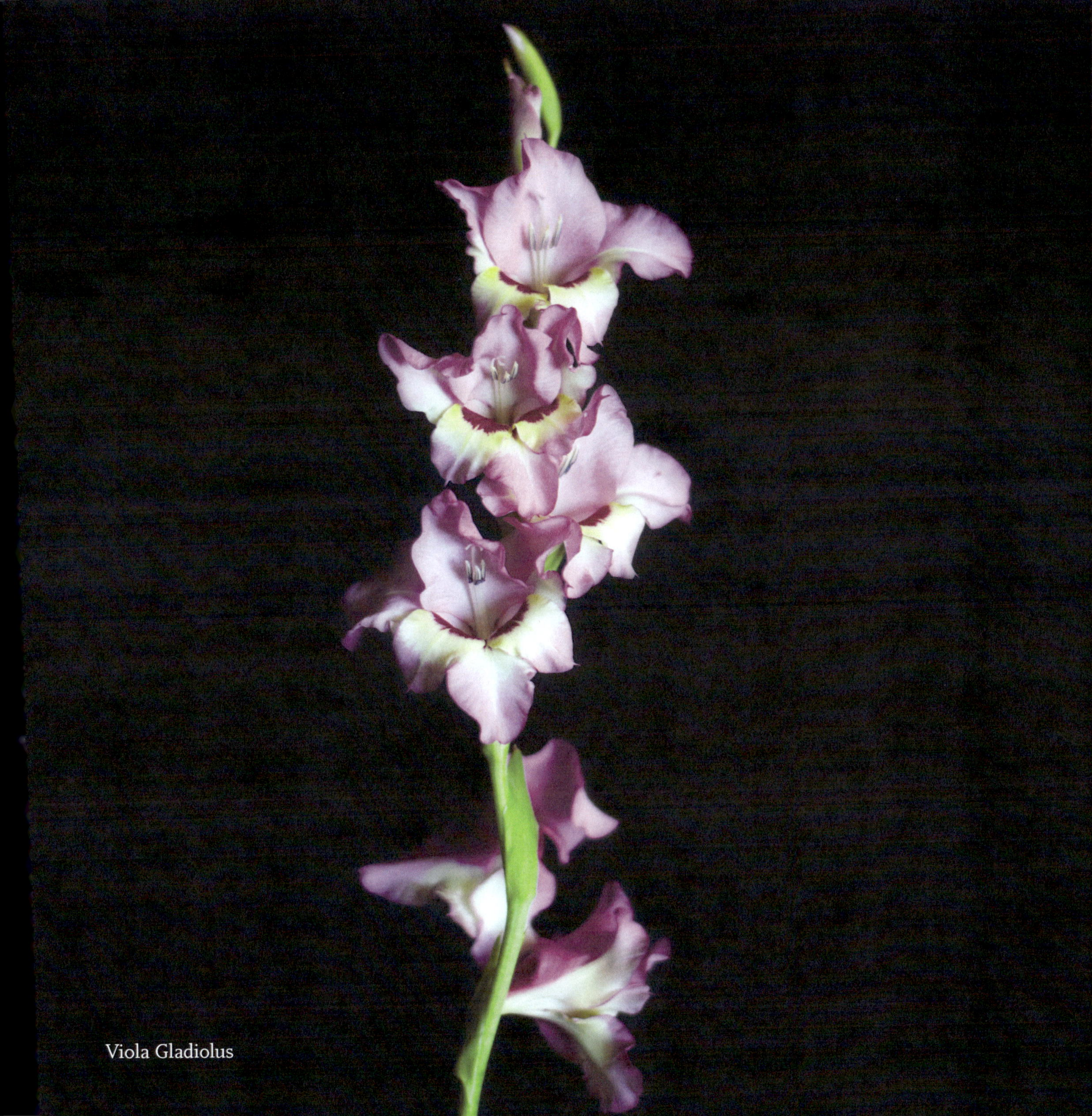
Viola Gladiolus

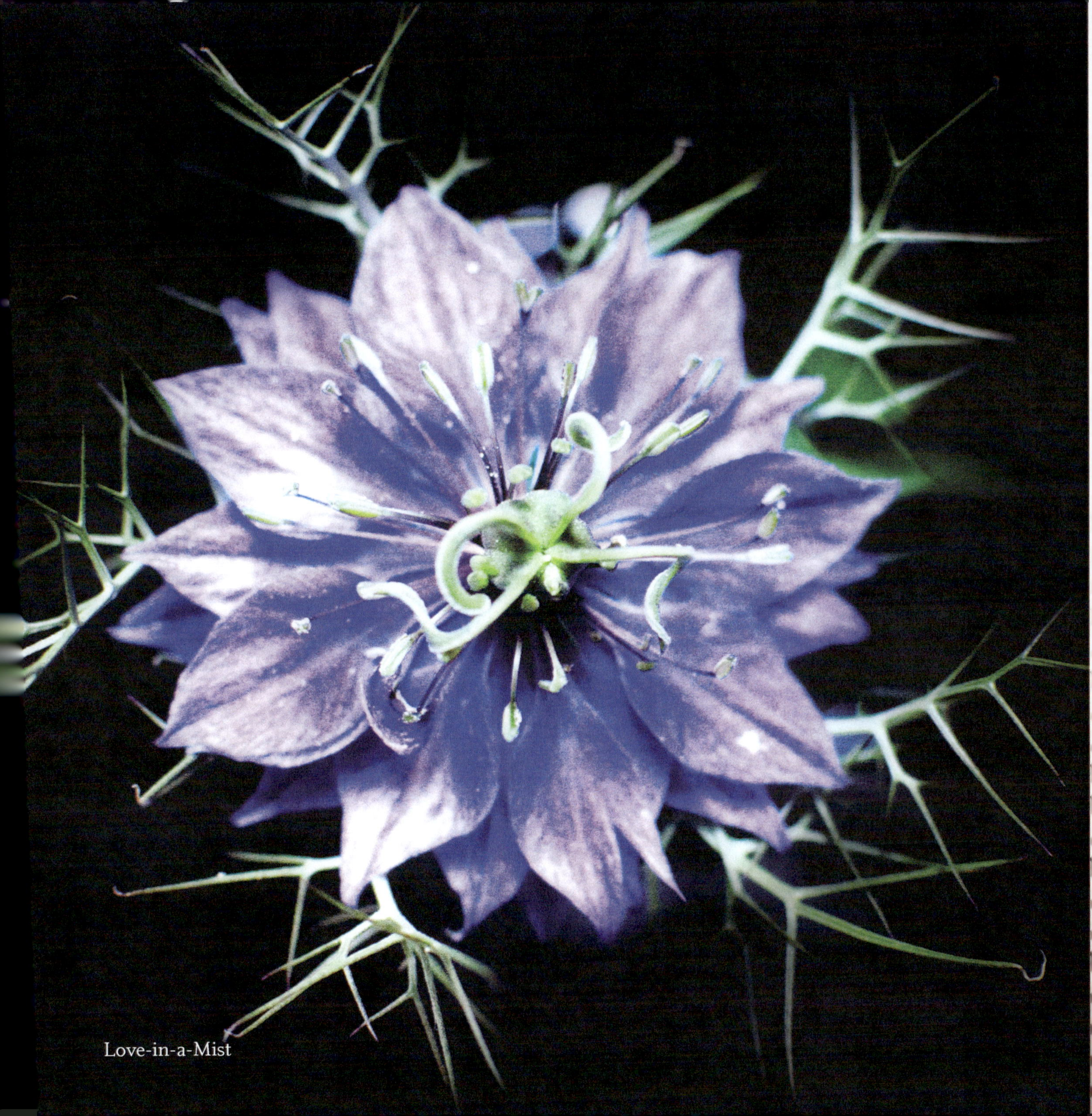

Love-in-a-Mist

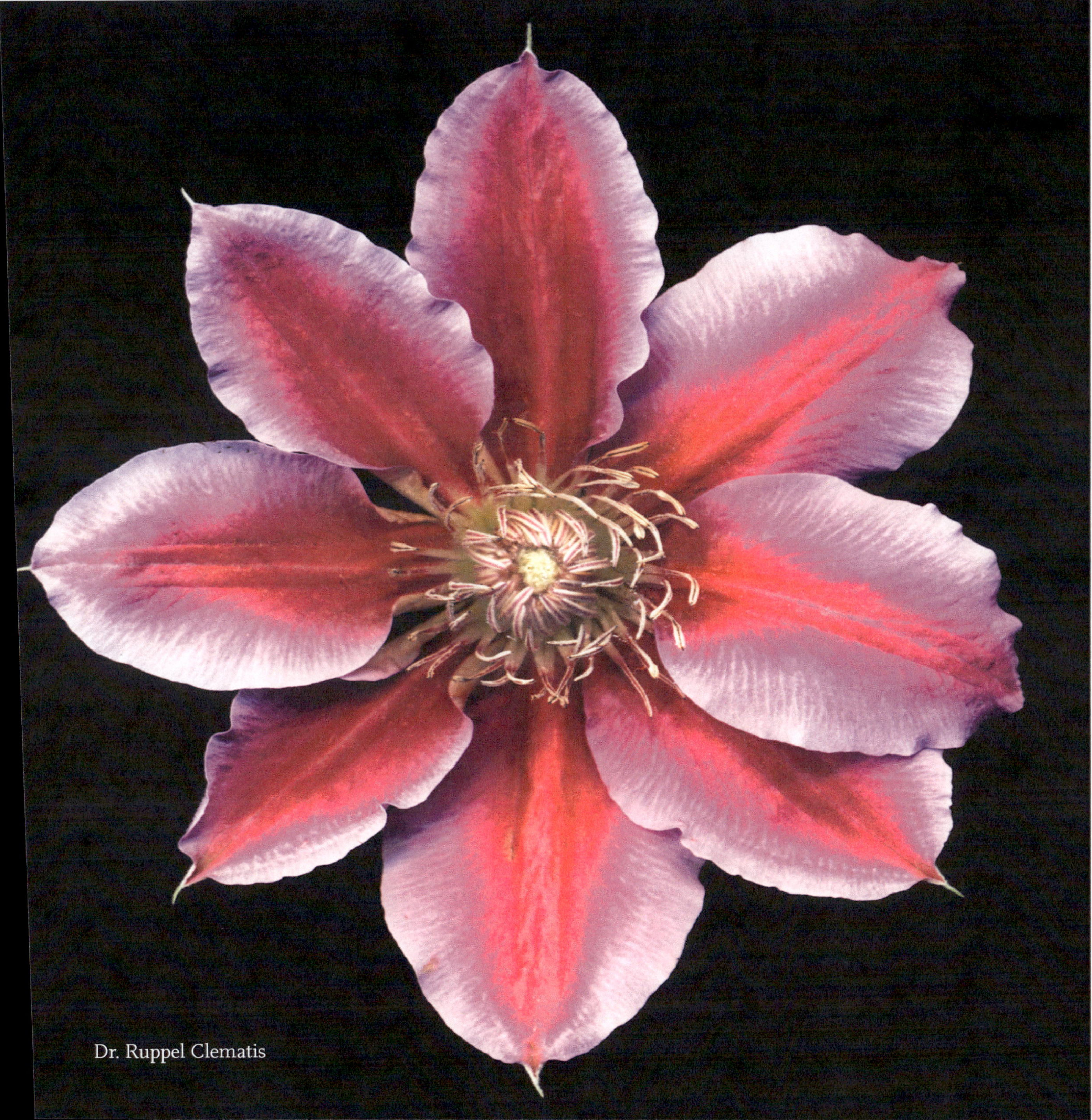

Dr. Ruppel Clematis

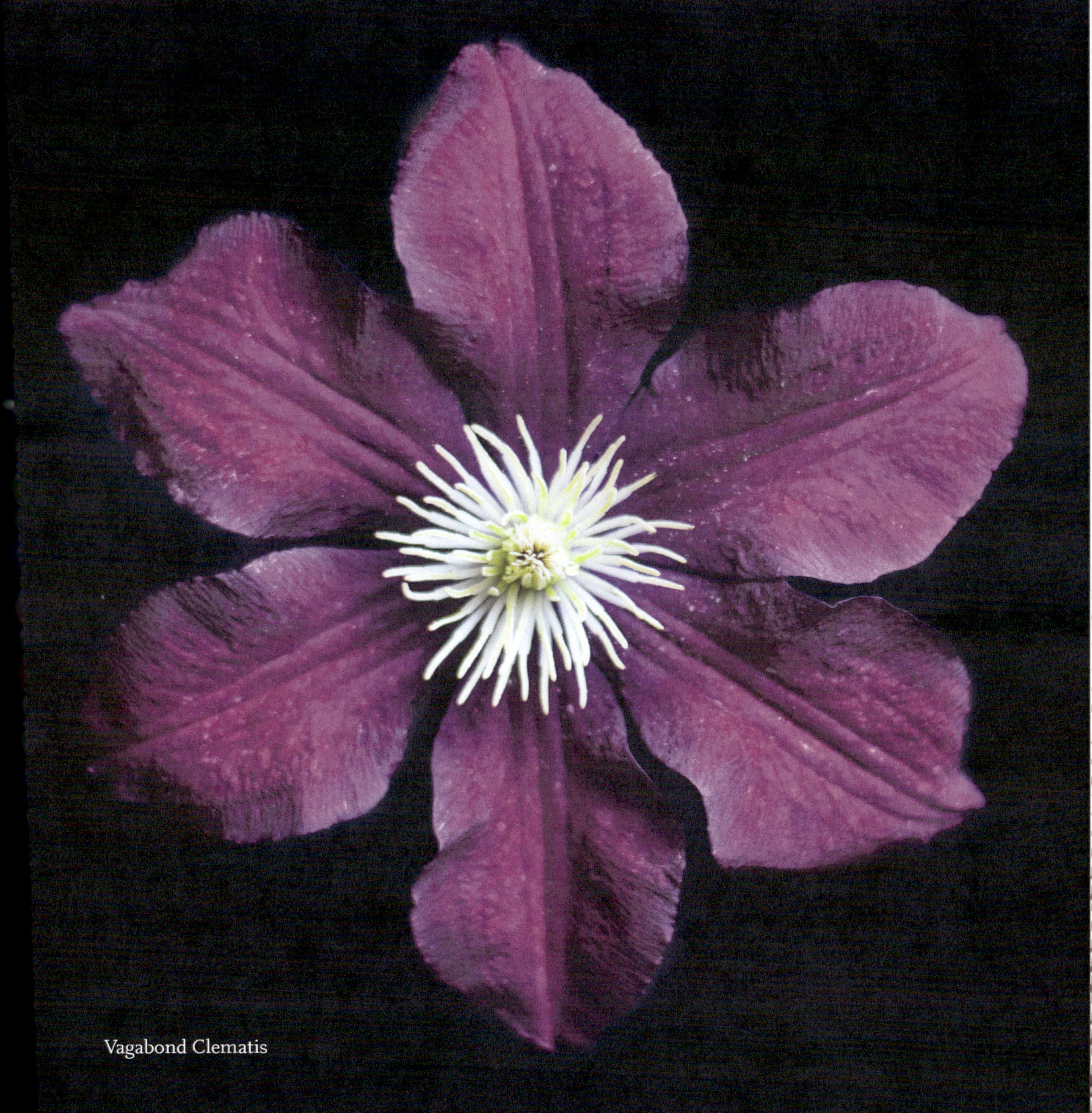

Vagabond Clematis

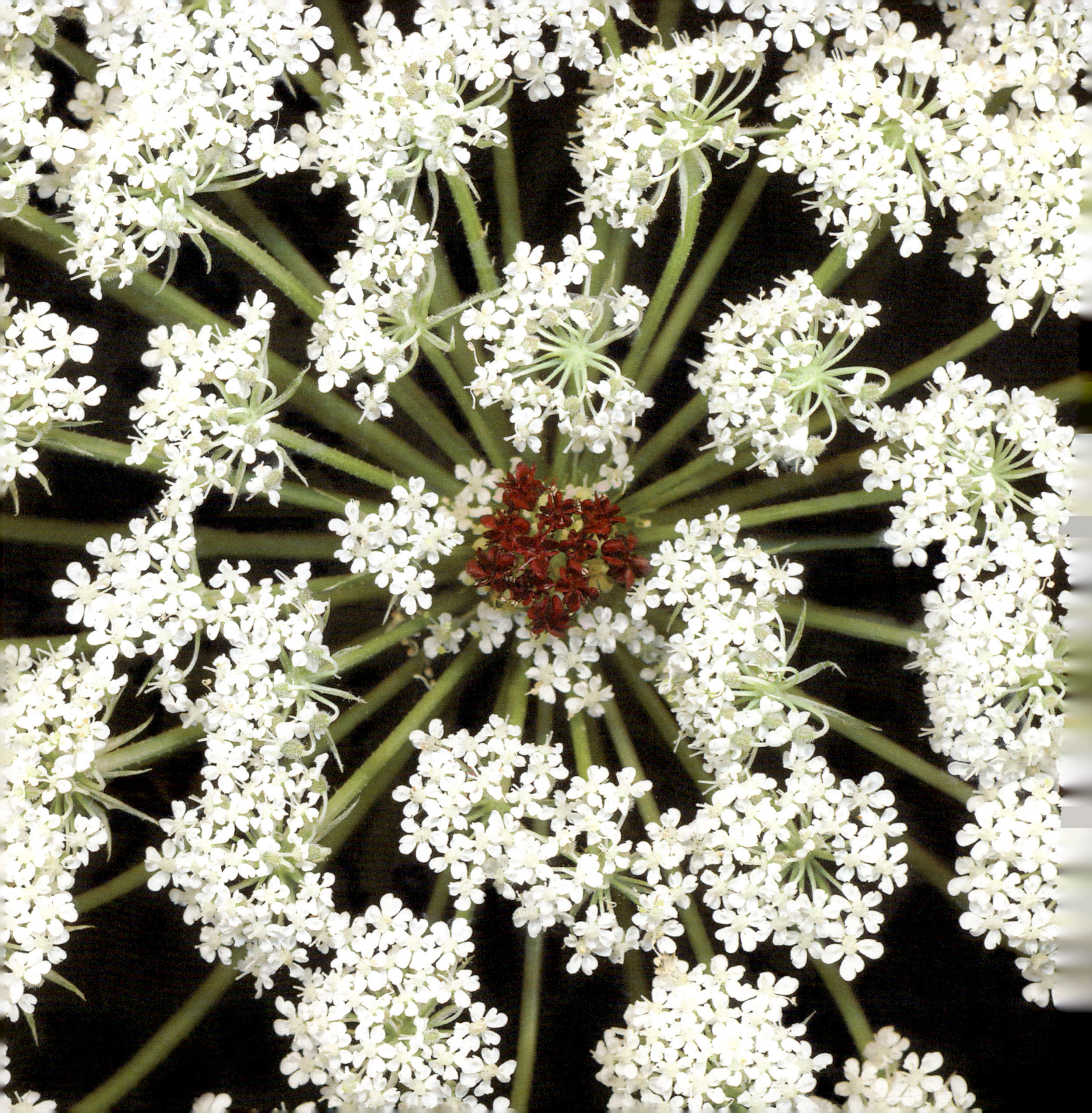

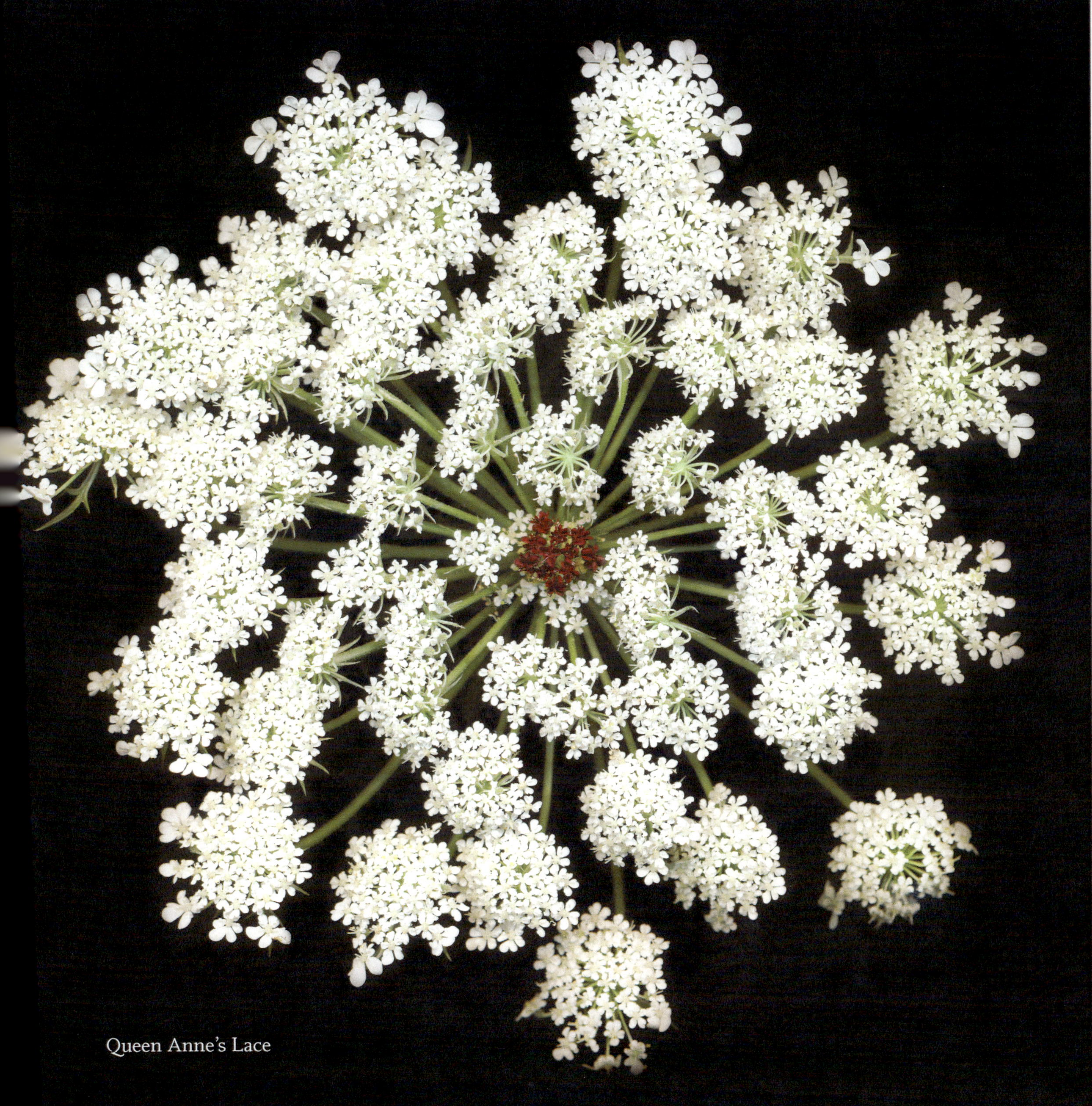

Queen Anne's Lace

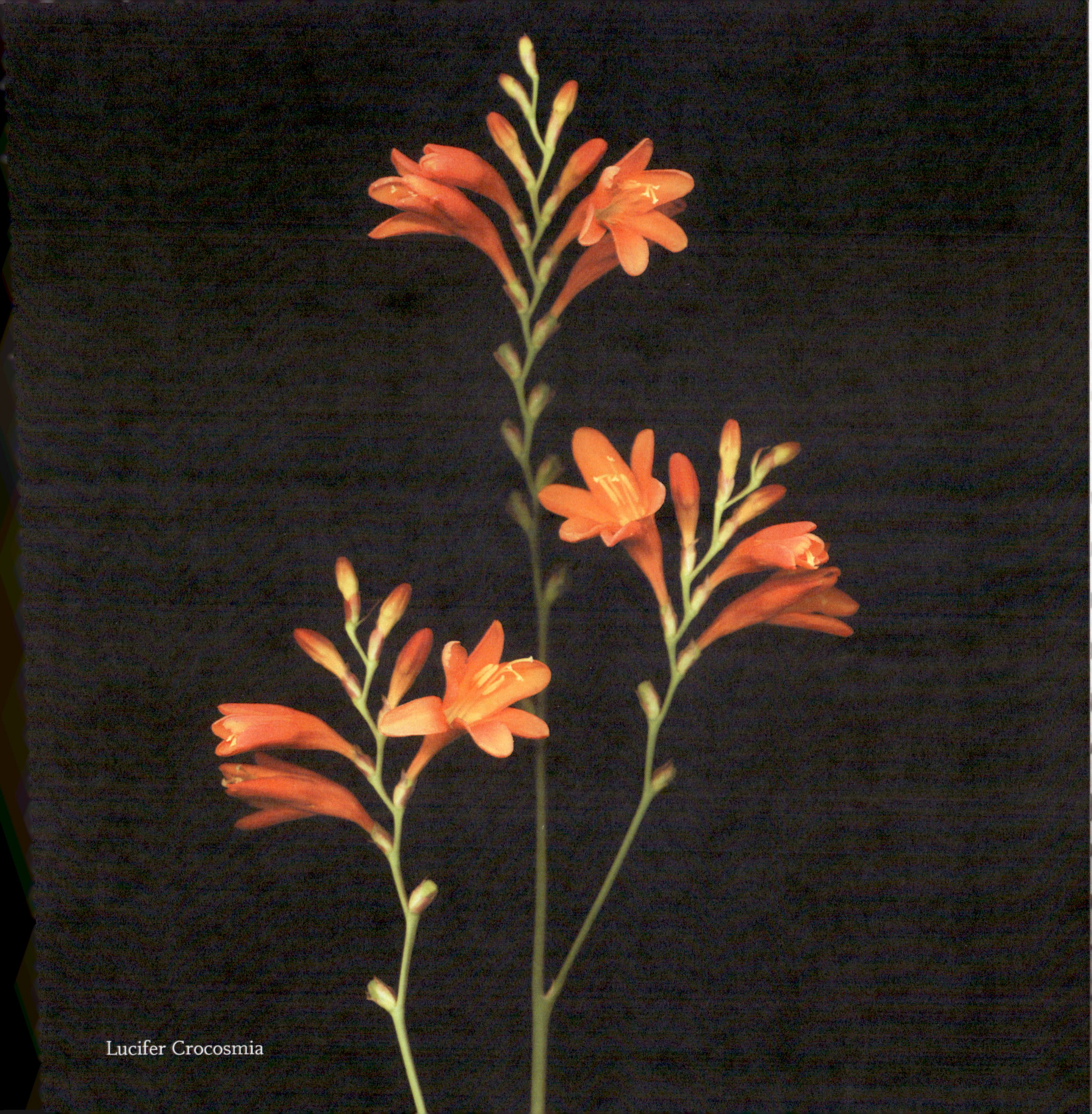
Lucifer Crocosmia

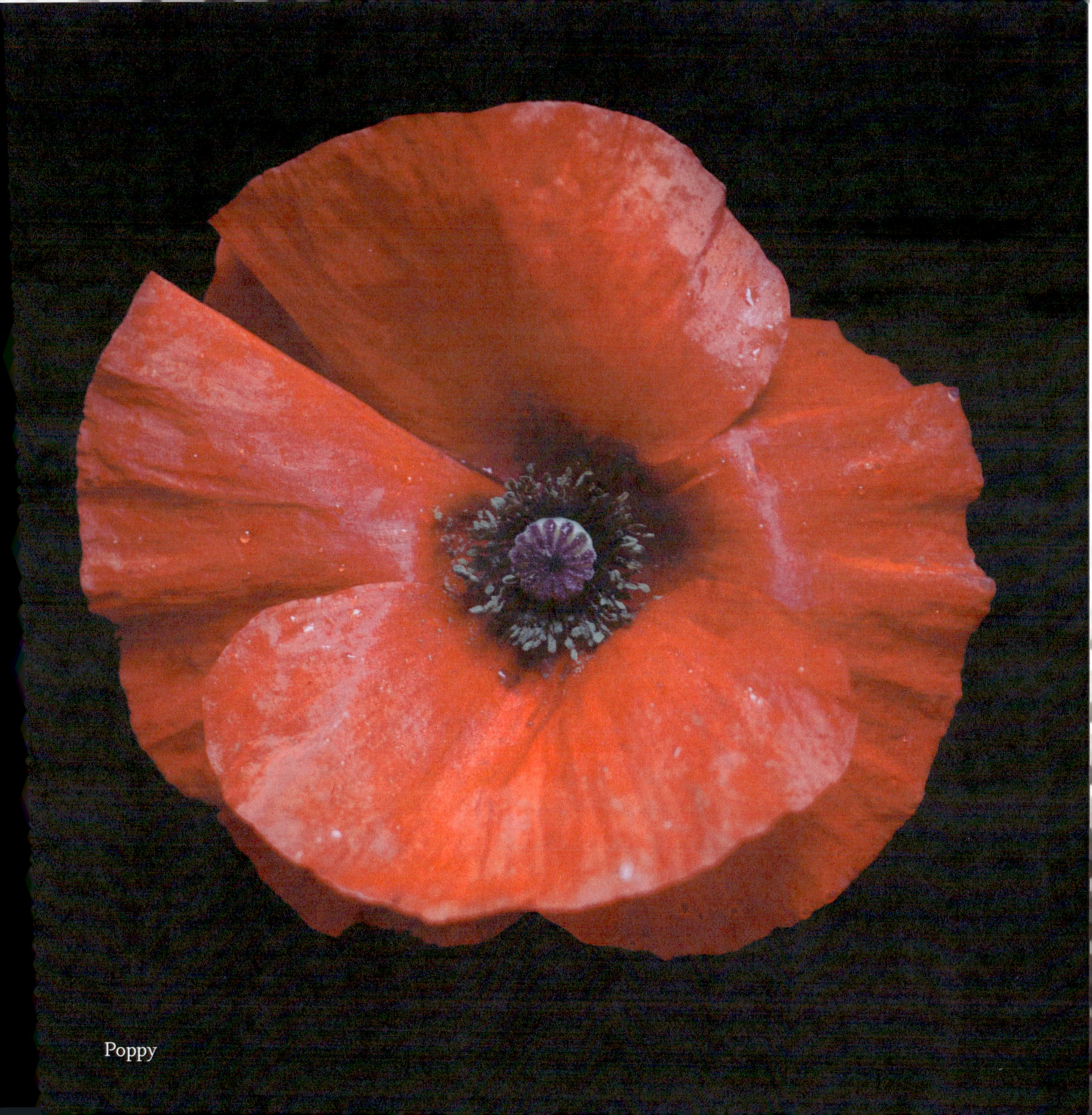
Poppy

9 798218 059125